TAWASSUL

its Types and its Rulings

Shaikh Muhammad Naasiruddeen al-Albaanee

Translated by
Aboo Talhah Daawood ibn Ronald Burbank

ISBN 1 898649 15 4

British Library Cataloguing in Publication Data.

A catalogue record for this book is available from the British Library.

First Edition, 1417 AH/1996 CE

© Copyright 1995 by Al-Hidaayah Publishing and Distribution Ltd.

Published by: Al-Hidaayah Publishing and Distribution

P.O. Box 3332

Birmingham

United Kingdom

B10 0UH

Tel: 0121 753 1889

Fax: 0121 753 2422

E-mail: mail@al-hidaayah.co.uk

PUBLISHER'S NOTE

All praise is for Allaah, Lord of the worlds. Peace and blessings of Allaah be upon Muhammad, his family, his Companions and all those who follow in their footsteps until the Last Day.

It gives us great pleasure in presenting "Tawassul - its Types and its Rulings" (the English translation of *At-Tawassul Anwaa'uhu wa Ahkaamuhu*) to the English readership, written by the great scholar of *Hadeeth* of our age Shaikh Muhammad Naasiruddeen al-Albaanee, may Allaah preserve him.

The meaning of *tawassul* is "a means of getting closer to Allaah." This book deals with the issue of *tawassul* and clarifies which forms of *tawassul* are permitted and which forms are invented by the people with no basis in the *sharee'ah*. For example, is it permissible to say as many Muslims say, "By the right of Muhammad (ﷺ) accept my supplication" or is this not allowed?

Shaikh al-Albaanee in his usual scholarly manner identifies the types of *tawassul* that are approved of in the Book of Allaah and the authentic *ahaadeeth* of the Messenger (ﷺ). He also goes to great lengths to show the falsity of the invented forms of *tawassul*, refuting the doubts that are raised one by one.

We pray that this book serves to remove the confusion and ignorance that the people are suffering from regarding this important issue, and that it will save some of His Slaves from falling into *Shirk - aameen.*

Al-Hidaayah Publishing and Distribution Ltd

CONTENTS

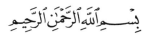

INTRODUCTION

All Praise and thanks are for Allaah, Lord of all the worlds and may He send praises and blessings upon the chief of all the Prophets and Messengers, and upon his family, his Companions and whoever follows his guidance until the Day of Judgement.

The basis for this treatise which I present to the noble readers are two lectures which our teacher Muhammad Naasirud-deen al-Albaanee delivered to a group of Muslim youth in the summer of 1392H, at his home in Yarmuk, camp in the city of Damascus. In them, he dealt with the topic of *at-Tawassul* and all its aspects, and researched it thoroughly, with the wide knowledge, sound discernment and precise investigation and checking which he is well known for; indeed it is rare that you find another like him in this age. Those present thought highly of the valuable study due to the sound scholarly research and its proofs which were strong and clear, and were convinced of its conclusions and the view arrived at by it, which is at the same time the position of the *mujtahid imaams* of the past, *rahimahumullaah*.

We saw that it contained immense benefit and there was a great need for its publication so that it could be made available to the Muslims, helping to release them from a great deal of confusion which they have about this topic. Furthermore, thanks for all bounties are due to Allaah who made this easy, since a number of brothers, recorded the lectures and one of the brothers who keenly strives to seek the knowledge, transcribed them in clear and beautiful handwriting, so may Allaah, the Most High, reward him well for that effort. Then I polished the text to make it suitable for publication and added some points of benefit where appropriate. I also provided the source references for the *Aayaat* and some of the *ahaadeeth* occurring in it. Then our teacher al-Albaanee retrieved a manuscript of a treatise which he had written almost twenty years previously entitled: *Tawassul and the Ahaadeeth about it*. This was one of a series called: *Attainment of a Sound Judgement about those who Claim to be Aiding the Rightly-Guided Khaleefahs and the Companions*. In this series he replied to a number of innovators and followers of falsehood who sought to attack the *Salafee da'wah* through various treatise in which they were guilty of falsehood and such blind attacks as do not in any way conform with knowledge and sincerity which is essential for it. So our teacher showed me that treatise, and I examined it, and found that it contained valuable points and extra benefits not found in the two lectures. I therefore added these where it was possible to do so, leaving out what was not needed. Then I presented the whole treatise in its new form to the author, may Allaah preserve him, and he refined and revised it in order to increase its clarity and usefulness. So this treatise, despite its brevity, is comprehensive, through Allaah's grace and grant of what is good, and I present it here to the noble readers hoping that they find a great deal of good in it and great benefit. Furthermore I ask the Generous Lord and Protector that He writes a great reward for its author, and its publisher, and all praise and thanks are for Allaah through whose blessings righteous deeds are completed. He is sufficient for us and the most excellent Disposer of affairs.

Damascus, 27th Rabee'ul-Awwal 1395H.
Corresponding to 19th April 1975.
Muhammad 'Eid al-'Abbaasee.

TAWASSUL - ITS TYPES AND RELATED RULINGS

All praise and thanks are for Allaah, we praise Him, seek His aid, and ask His forgiveness. We seek Allaah's refuge from the evils of our own selves and from our evil actions. Whomever Allaah guides none can misguide him, and whomever Allaah leads astray then none can guide him. I testify that none has the right to be worshipped except Allaah, alone, having no partner, and I testify that Muhammad is His slave and His Messenger.

يَـٰٓأَيُّهَا ٱلَّذِينَ ءَامَنُوا۟ ٱتَّقُوا۟ ٱللَّهَ حَقَّ تُقَاتِهِۦ وَلَا تَمُوتُنَّ إِلَّا وَأَنتُم مُّسْلِمُونَ ۝

"O you who believe! Fear Allaah as He should be feared and die not except in a state of *Islaam* with complete submission to Allaah."[1]

يَـٰٓأَيُّهَا ٱلنَّاسُ ٱتَّقُوا۟ رَبَّكُمُ ٱلَّذِى خَلَقَكُم مِّن نَّفْسٍ وَٰحِدَةٍ وَخَلَقَ مِنْهَا زَوْجَهَا وَبَثَّ مِنْهُمَا رِجَالًا كَثِيرًا وَنِسَآءً وَٱتَّقُوا۟ ٱللَّهَ ٱلَّذِى تَسَآءَلُونَ بِهِۦ وَٱلْأَرْحَامَ إِنَّ ٱللَّهَ كَانَ عَلَيْكُمْ رَقِيبًا ۝

"O mankind! Be dutiful to your Lord, Who created you from a single person (Aadam), and from him (Aadam) He created his wife (Eve), and from them both He created many men and women and fear Allaah through whom you demand your mutual (rights), and (do not cut the relations of) the wombs (kinship). Surely, Allaah is Ever an all Watcher over you."[2]

---

1. Soorah Aali-'Imraan (3): 102
2. Soorah An-Nisaa (4): 1

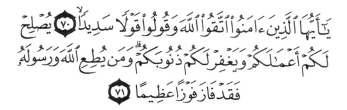

"O you who believe! Keep your duty to Allaah and fear
Him, and speak (always) the truth. He will direct you to
do righteous good deeds and will forgive you your sins.
And whosoever obeys Allaah and His Messenger (ﷺ) he
has indeed achieved a great achievement."[3]

Indeed the best speech is the Book of Allaah, and the best way is the way of
Muhammad. The worst of affairs are novelties, every novelty is an innovation,
every innovation is misguidance, and all misguidance is in the Fire.

The people are in great confusion about the matter of *Tawassul* and its rulings
in the religion, and they greatly differ concerning it, some declaring it lawful
and others prohibiting it, some going to extremes and others being over-
lenient. Also, a large number of the Muslims have for centuries been used to
saying in their supplications such things as: 'O Allaah by the right of your
Prophet...,' or 'by the right of the Sacred House... forgive me.' and 'O Allaah by
the right of the *Awliyaa* and the pious, and so and so, etc.' or 'O Allaah by the
honour of the men of Allaah to You, and by the honour of those in whose presence we are, and under whose assistance we exist[4], relieve us and the distressed from all distress.'

Also: 'O Allaah we humbly beseech You with outstretched hands, seeking a

---

3. Soorah Al-Ahzaab (33): 70-71

4. The belief that any deceased person gives any help or assistance is a futile and false belief,
and seeking for such help from them is to call upon others besides Allaah for aid, and this is one
of the types of Major *Shirk* (*ash-Shirkul-Akbar*), and we seek Allaah's refuge from that.

means of *waseelah* to You through the one deserving of *waseelah* and inter-cession, that you aid *Islaam* and the Muslims.' etc. They call this '*waseelah*' and they claim that it is permissible and something prescribed in the *Sharee'ah*[5] and that it is affirmed and prescribed in a number of *Aayaat* and *abaadeeth*, indeed that these texts order and encourage it. Some people even go so far beyond bounds that they even allow *tawassul* to Allaah, the Most High, through some inanimate objects from the creation that do not even reach the level of the aforementioned, such as graves of the *Awliyaa*, metal structures built upon their tombs, and earth, stones and trees found nearby. They claim that whatever is near to those who are honoured itself becomes honoured, and that the honour which Allaah bestows upon the occupant of a grave passes on to the grave itself, so that *it* becomes a means of *Waseelah* to draw nearer to Allaah thereby. Indeed some of the later people allow directly seeking aid from others besides Allaah! So what is *Tawassul*? What are its types? What is the meaning of the *Aayaat* and the *abaadeeth* which mention it? And what is the correct ruling for it in *Islaam*?

---

5. Translator's note: The Islamic system and law covering all aspects of life.

Tawassul in the Arabic Language and in the Qur'aan

THE MEANING OF TAWASSUL IN THE ARABIC LANGUAGE

Before going into this topic in detail I would like to draw attention to an important reason why many people have an incorrect understanding of the meaning of *Tawassul*, and why they go beyond bounds with regard to it and enter into it things which are not from it. The reason is their lack of understanding of its meaning in the language and their lack of knowledge of it from its original root meaning. This is that the word *Tawassul* is an original Arabic word occurring in the Qur'aan and *Sunnah* and in ancient Arabic poetry and prose, and its meaning is: *To draw near to what one seeks after and to approach that which one desires.* Ibnul-Atheer said in *an-Nihaayah*: "*Al-Waasil* is one who desires or longs for something, and *al-Waseelah* is nearness and a means, and that by which one is able to approach and draw near to something. Its plural is *Wasaail*." Al-Fayroozabaadee said in *al-Qaamoos*: "'He performed *waseelah* towards Allaah, the Most High,' means: He did an action in order to draw nearer to Him, as a means of approaching Him." Ibn Faaris said in *Mu'jamul Maqaayees*: "*Waseelah* is to desire and to seek after. One says *Waslas* for one who wishes and aspires for something, and the *Waasil* is the one who wishes to draw nearer to Allaah, the Mighty and Majestic, and it occurs in the saying of Labeed: 'I see that the people do not know the value of their affair, whereas every religious person seeks to draw nearer to Allaah.'"

Ar-Raaghib al-Asfahaanee said in *al-Mufradaat*: "*Al-Waseelah* (written with the letter س) is to approach that which one desires, and it is more particular than *al-Waseelah* (written with the letter ص) since it includes the concept of being desirous of it. Allaah, the Most High, says:

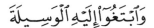

"Seek the means of approach (*al-waseelah*) to Him"[6]

The reality of seeking a *waseelah* to Allaah, the Most High, is: To take care to follow His way with (good) actions and worship, by adhering to the noble qualities required in the *Sharee'ah*. It is like nearness, and the *waasil* is one who aspires nearness to Allaah, the Most High."

The famous scholar Ibn Jareer also reports this meaning and then brings as evidence the saying of the poet: "If the informers miss us then we will arrive, and the relations and the means of approach (*waseelah*) between us will be restored."

Then there is another meaning for *waseelah* and it is rank and standing with a king and closeness to him. Just as in the *hadeeth*, it is the name given to the highest station in Paradise, in his (ﷺ) saying: *When you hear the caller to Prayer then say the like of what he says, then send blessings (salaat) upon me, since whoever sends a single blessing upon me then Allaah will send ten upon*

---

6. Soorah Al-Maaidah (5):35

him because of it. Then ask Allaah to grant me al-waseelah because it is a station in Paradise which is appropriate only for a single servant from the servants of Allaah, and I hope that it will be me. So whoever asks for al-waseelah to be granted to me then my intercession is due for him.[7]

As is clear, the last two meanings for *waseelah* are closely connected to its original meaning, however they are not what is meant in this treatise of ours.

THE MEANING OF *WASEELAH* IN THE *QUR'AAN*

What we have presented so far is the meaning that is well-known in the language, and nobody disagrees about that. It is also the meaning given by the Pious Predecessors (*as-Salafus-Saalih*) and the *imaams* of *tafseer* in explanation of the two *Aayaat* in which the word *al-waseelah* occurs. They are the Saying of Allaah, the Most High:

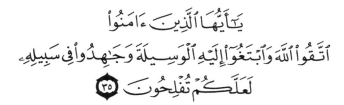

"O you who believe! Do your duty to Allaah and fear Him. Seek the means of approach (*al-waseelah*) to Him, and strive hard in His Cause as much as you can. So that you may be successful."[8]

---

7. Reported by Muslim (translation 1/209/no.747), the four *Sunan* and others and it is brought in my book *Irwaaul-Ghaleel* (no.242).

8. Soorah Al-Maaidah (5):35

أُوْلَئِكَ ٱلَّذِينَ

يَدْعُونَ يَبْتَغُونَ إِلَىٰ رَبِّهِمُ ٱلْوَسِيلَةَ أَيُّهُمْ أَقْرَبُ وَيَرْجُونَ

رَحْمَتَهُۥ وَيَخَافُونَ عَذَابَهُۥٓ إِنَّ عَذَابَ رَبِّكَ كَانَ مَحْذُورًا ٥٧

"Those whom they call upon (like Jesus son of Mary, Ezra etc.) desire (for themselves) means of access (*al-waseelah*) to their Lord (Allaah), as to which of them should be nearest and they (Jesus, Ezra, angels, etc.) hope for His Mercy and fear His Torment. Verily, the Torment of your Lord is somethng to be afraid of!"[9]

As for the first *Aayah* then the *imaam* of the scholars of *tafseer* al-Haafidh Ibn Jareer [at-Tabaree], *rahimahullaah*, said in explanation of it: "O you who affirm whatever Allaah and His Messenger inform you of, and affirm whatever reward He promised and whatever punishment He threatened, ٱتَّقُوا ٱللَّهَ: **"Fear Allaah."** He says: Respond to Allaah by obeying Him regarding whatever He has ordered or forbidden. وَٱبْتَغُوٓا إِلَيْهِ ٱلْوَسِيلَةَ : **"and Seek a Means of approach to Him."** He says: And seek to draw near to Him by doing actions which are pleasing to Him."

Al-Haafidh Ibn Katheer reports from Ibn 'Abbaas, *radiyallaahu 'anhumaa*, that the meaning of *waseelah* is to draw closer. He also reports the like of that from Mujaahid, Aboo Waail, al-Hasan, 'Abdullaah ibn Katheer, as-Suddee, Ibn Zayd and others. He also reports from Qataadah that he said about it: "That is: that you draw near to Him by obedience to Him and through action that is pleasing to Him." Then Ibn Katheer said: "And with regard to what those *imaams* said there is no disagreement between the scholars of *tafseer* about it... and *al-waseelah* is that by means of which one reaches that which he

---

9. Soorah Al-Israa (17): 57

desires."[10]

As for the second *Aayah*, then the distinguished Companion 'Abdullaah ibn Mas'ood, *radiyallaahu 'anhu*, explained the circumstances in which it was sent down, which clarifies its meaning. He said: "It was sent down concerning a group of Arabs who used to worship a group of *Jinn*, then the *Jinns* accepted *Islaam* unknown to the people who worshipped them."[11]

Al-Haafidh Ibn Hajr, *rahimahullaah*,[12]said: "That is the people who used to worship the *Jinn* continued to worship the *Jinn*, and the *Jinn* were not pleased with that since they had accepted *Islaam*, and they were the ones who sought a means of nearness to their Lord, this is what is reliable with regard to *tafseer* of the *Aayah*."

This is very clear that what is meant by the *waseelah* is those actions by which one draws nearer to Allaah, the Most High, therefore He said: يَبْتَغُونَ : **"they seek"** i.e. they seek to do such righteous actions as will bring them closer to Allaah, the Most High. It also clearly shows the very strange case - contrary to sound and unblemished thinking - that some people direct their worship and their supplication to some of the servants of Allaah, fearing them and placing hope in them, despite the fact that those servants whom they are worshipping have themselves openly declared their *Islaam* and their servitude to and their worship of Allaah, and they have hastened to perform deeds to bring them nearer to Him, the One free of all imperfections, performing righteous deeds which He loves and is pleased with, hoping for His mercy and fearing His punishment. So Allaah, the Most Perfect, declares the foolishness of the empty

---

10. *Tafseer Ibn Katheer* (2/52-53).

11. Reported by Muslim (translation 4/1555/no.7182) and its like is reported by al-Bukhaaree (translation 6/202/no.238) and in a wording of his: "So the *Jinns* accepted *Islaam* but those people remained upon their religion."

12. In *Fathul-Baaree* (10/12&13).

hopes of those ignorant people who worshipped the *Jinn* and continued to worship them despite the fact that they were themselves created beings and worshippers of Allaah and weak and powerless before Him, just like the humans themselves. They did not possess any benefit or harm for themselves, and Allaah rebukes those people for not directing their worship to Him alone, the Blessed and Most High, since He alone is the One who controls harm and benefit, and in His Hand is the control and protection of everything.

RIGHTEOUS ACTIONS ALONE ARE THE *WASEELAH* WHICH DRAW ONE CLOSER TO ALLAAH

It is also very strange that some of those who claim to have knowledge have become accustomed to using these two *Aayaat* as an evidence for what many of them are fervently attached to with regard to seeking *tawassul* through the persons of the prophets, or their honour, or their status, and this is erroneous and the two *Aayaat* cannot be used to support it, since it is not established in the *Sharee'ah* that this *tawassul* is prescribed and desirable. What they understand from these *Aayaat* is that Allaah, the Blessed and Most High, orders us to draw nearer to Him fervently and to seek a means of nearness to Him by doing deeds of righteousness, and to seek closeness to Him by any means.

However Allaah, the One free of all imperfections, teaches us in many other texts that if we seek to draw closer to Him them we must do so by performing righteous deeds which are pleasing to Him. He did not leave those actions up to us, nor did He leave it up to our intellect and our tastes and feelings to decide which actions they should be, since in that case we would disagree and differ, conflict and argue. Rather He, the One free of all imperfections, ordered us to refer to Him for that and to follow His guidance and teaching about that. This is because no one knows what pleases Allaah, the Mighty and Majestic, except Him alone. Therefore in order for us to know the means to draw nearer to Allaah, it is obligatory upon us to refer back, in every matter, to that which Allaah, the Most Perfect, prescribed in the *Sharee'ah*, and which Allaah's Messenger (ﷺ) explained. The meaning of this is that we refer back to the

Book of Allaah and the *Sunnah* of His Messenger ( ). Indeed this is what our
Messenger Muhammad ( ) commanded us to do in his saying: *I have left
amongst you two things; you will not go astray as long as you cling to them:
The Book of Allaah and the Sunnah of His Messenger*.[13]

WHEN IS AN ACTION A RIGHTEOUS ACTION

It is made clear in the Book and the *Sunnah* that for an action to be a 'righteous action' and for it to be acceptable to Allaah, the One free of all imperfections, and one which draws a person closer to Him, then it must fulfil two
important conditions:

T h e   f i r s t is that the intention of the person doing it must be sincerely
for the sake of Allaah.
T h e   s e c o n d is that it must be in accordance with what Allaah, the
Blessed and Most High, prescribed in His Book and what His Messenger
explained in his *Sunnah*.

If one of these two conditions is absent then the action is neither a righteous
action nor is it acceptable. This is indicated by the Saying of Allaah, the Blessed
and the Most High:

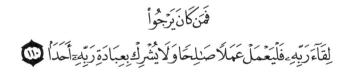

**"So whoever hopes for the meeting with his Lord, let
him work righteousness and associate none as a partner
in the worship of his Lord."**[14]

---

13. Reported by Maalik in *mursal* form, and by al-Haakim from the *hadeeth* of Ibn 'Abbaas
with *hasan* chain of narration. It also has a witness in the *hadeeth* of Jaabir which I quote in
Silsilatus-Saheehah (no.1761).

14. Soorah Al-Kahf (18): 110

So He, the One free of all imperfections, orders that the actions should be 'righteous', that is in accordance with the *Sunnah*. Then He orders that it should be done purely for Him and not for any other incentive. Al-Haafidh Ibn Katheer said in his *Tafseer*: "These two things are the two pillars of an acceptable action, it must be done purely for Allaah, and done correctly in the manner prescribed in the *Sharee'ah* of Allaah's Messenger (ﷺ)." This is also reported from al-Qadee 'Iyaad, *rahimahullaah*, and others.

chapter TWO

Natural Means and Means Prescribed for Goals in the *Sharee'ah*[15]

When we know that *al-waseelah* is the means by which we are able to reach the goal we desire, then we should know that they are of two categories: natural means and means prescribed in the *Sharee'ah*. As for the natural means, then it is every natural means through which a person attains that which is desired, being known to him through the innate nature upon which Allaah created him. This is common to both the Believer and the Unbeliever, with no difference between them. Examples of it are water, which is a means to quench a persons thirst; food, which is a means to satisfy hunger; clothes, which are a means to preserve him from heat and cold; cars, which are a means of moving him from place to place, and so on.

---

15. i.e. things ordered or encouraged in the religion which earn Allaah's pleasure and lead to Paradise.

As for the means prescribed for the goals in the *Sharee'ah* then they are every way of reaching that which is desired, by way of that which Allaah, the Most High, prescribed and explained in His Book and in the *Sunnah* of His Messenger. This is particular to the Believer who follows and is obedient to the orders of Allaah and His Messenger. Examples of this are: Saying the two testifications of Faith with purity of intention and understanding, since that is the means to obtain entry into Paradise and to be saved from dwelling eternally in the Hell-Fire. Likewise following up an evil deed with a good deed is a means to wipe away the evil deed. Also supplicating with the prescribed supplication after the *adhaan* is a means of gaining the intercession of the Prophet(ﷺ), and keeping ties of relationship is a means for a long lifespan and increased provision and so on.

So these things and their like are known to us to be means to attain those goals, being known as such from the *Sharee'ah* alone, not being known by means of our personal knowledge, experience or our senses. So we cannot know that keeping ties of relationship is a means for a long lifespan and ample provision except from the words of Allaah's Messenger (ﷺ): *Whoever loves that increase in provision should be granted to him, and that he should be granted long life, then let him keep ties of relationship.*[16] And likewise with the other examples. Many people make a great error in their understanding of these two types of means. Some think that something is a natural means to attain a certain goal, whereas this is not the case. Others believe something to be a *Sharee'ah* - prescribed means to reach some goal in the *Sharee'ah* whereas in truth what they believe is not true.

So from the examples of false and futile means, both in the natural and *Sharee'ah* sense at one and the same time, are (for example), something which one who walks in Nasr street in Damascus will see very often: that a person sets

---

16.   Reported by al-Bukhaaree (translation 8/11/no.14) and Muslim (translation 4/1359/no.6202) and others.

up a small table and on it there is a small animal like a mouse. Next to it they place a pile of small cards containing some writing which they claim to be the peoples fortunes - the writing on the cards is written by they themselves or by someone else based on their ignorance. So two close friends will be walking along and one will say to the other: 'Lets go and see what our fortunes are.' So they give some coins to the man and he lets the little animal choose a card and give it to one of them to read. He then reads what is claimed to be his fortune! So you see the level of intelligence of these people who take an animal as a guide to show them these things which they are ignorant of, and to inform them about their destiny which is concealed from them! If he actually believes that this animal knows the unseen and hidden matters then there is no doubt that the animal is better than he is! If however he does not believe this, then it is a useless and foolish waste of time and money, which would not be indulged in by people of intelligence. Likewise the action itself is a swindle and mis-guidance and a means of devouring the peoples wealth in futility. There is no doubt that the people turning to this animal in order to find out the unseen and hidden affairs is, according to their claims, a natural means. However it is futile and useless and experience and intellect demolishes it, since it is clearly only thought to be such due to superstition, ignorance and fraud. Then from the perspective of the *Sharee'ah* it is also false and futile since it is contrary to the Book, the *Sunnah* and the consensus (*ijmaa'*) of the scholars. Sufficient in this regard is that it contradicts the Saying of Allaah, the One free of all imperfections, in praise of Himself:

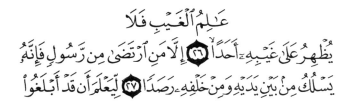

"(He alone is) the All-Knower of the unseen, and He reveals to none His unseen. Except to a Messenger (from

mankind) whom He has chosen (He informs him of the unseen as much as He likes)."[17]

Likewise from those things which some people incorrectly think are a natural means is that if one of them travels or marries on 'Wednesday' then his journey will be unsuccessful and the marriage will fail. Likewise their belief that if they begin something important and then see a blind man or something afflicted, that there work will not be completed and will be unsuccessful!

Also from the things which many Arabs and Muslims today think to be such means is the idea that by large numbers of men alone they can gain victory over the zionist and imperialist enemies, and that in their present state they will be able to force the Jews into the sea. However experience has shown the error and futility of these thoughts, and that the matter is more profound than to be cured by such superficial thinking.

Also from the things which they incorrectly imagine to be means prescribed in the *Sharee'ah* are those actions which some people think will draw them closer to Allaah, the One free of all imperfections, whereas in reality these actions only take them further away from Allaah and earn His Anger and Wrath for them. Indeed His curse and punishment. From these actions is that some of them call upon the deceased *awliyaa** and pious occupants of graves for assistance, requesting them to fulfil needs which can only be fulfilled by Allaah, the One free of all imperfections and the Most High. For example, requesting them to remove distress and cure illness, to bring provision and remove barrenness, and to grant them victory over their enemies and so on. For this aim, they wipe the metal railings upon tombs and the stones of graves, or they cast scraps of

---

17. Soorah Al-Jinn (72): 26-27.

* Publisher's Note: *Awliyaa* is plural of *walee*, meaning 'friend (of Allaah)' refering to someone pious. A *walee* can only be someone who is established upon the *Sunnah* of the Prophet (ﷺ).

paper into them upon which they have written their needs and desires. All of these are claimed by them to be means prescribed in the *Sharee'ah*, however they are in reality false and futile, and contrary to the greatest foundation of *Islaam*, which is that all worship is to be for Allaah, the Most High, alone, and that He is to be singled out with all the types and branches of worship.

Also from them is the belief of some of them that a person must be telling the truth if he or someone present sneezes whilst he is speaking.[18]

Likewise is their belief that if they hear a buzzing noise in their ear they think that one of their companions or relatives are saying something good about them.[19]

Also their belief that misfortune will descend upon them if they cut their nails at night, or on 'Saturday' or 'Sunday,'[20] or the same if they sweep their hous-

---

18. Perhaps the source for this belief is the *hadeeth*: *Whoever says something and sneezes whilst saying it, then it is true.* Ash-Shawkaanee quotes it in his book of fabricated narrations *Al-Fawaaidul Majmoo'ah fil -Ahaadeethil-Mawdoo'ah* (p.224). This and the following example are a sufficient proof of the danger of weak and fabricated *ahaadeeth* and their effect upon the spread of false beliefs and baseless habits. So this necessitates that every Muslim should be aware of them and warn against them. This cannot be achieved except through giving attention and careful study to the sciences of *hadeeth*. This is what lead me to compile the book: *Silsilatul-Ahaadeeth-Da'eefah wal-Mawdoo'ah wa Atharuhas-Sayyi fil-Ummah* [*The Series of Weak and Fabricated Hadeeth and the evil effect they have within the Ummah*]. You will find this *hadeeth* in it (no.136) along with an explanation of its baselessness.

19. The origin of this belief is a fabricated *hadeeth* with the wording: *If the ear of one of you buzzes then let him send blessings upon me and say: 'May Allaah mention the one who mentions me with good.'"* Ash-Shawkaanee brings it in *al-Fawaaidul-Majmoo'ah* (no.224).

20. Some people having some degree of knowledge took on this false belief and wrote it down in a poem which is taught to students in some schools of *Sharee'ah*.

es at night, and from these things is if they have good thoughts and intentions about a rock, then it will be of benefit to them.[21]

So these false beliefs and their like, indeed these superstitions and false nonsense, suppositions and delusions are things for which Allaah sent down no authority, and you have seen that they have their origin in fabricated and false *abaadeeth*, may Allaah's curse be upon those who fabricate them and may He disfigure those who invented them. So we know that natural means are divided between things which are lawful and permitted by Allaah, and things which are prohibited and forbidden by Allaah. In what has preceded I have given examples of the two types of means [natural and *Sharee'ah* prescribed] and about which the people fall into error, thinking that some things are lawful and practical means to attain the desired goal, whereas they are just the opposite. I will mention in what follows some examples of natural means which are allowed in the *Sharee'ah* and others which are not.

So from the natural means which are allowed in the *Sharee'ah* for earning a living and gaining provision are buying and selling; trade; agriculture and hiring out. Then from the natural but forbidden means are: giving loans to be repaid with the addition of usury (*ribaa*); disguised forms of usury; monopolies; deception; theft; gambling and sale of wine and statues. From the proofs of this is the Saying of Allaah, the Most High:

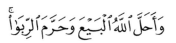

"Allaah has permitted trading and forbidden Ribaa."[22]

---

21. The origin of this belief of misguidance is a false *hadeeth*: *If one of you were to make his thoughts about a rock good then Allaah would cause it to be of benefit to him*. Al-Haafidh al-'Ajloonee quotes it in *Khashful-Khafaa* (2/152) and quotes Ibn Taymiyyah as saying that it is a lie, and from Ibn Hajr that there is no basis for it, and from the author of *al-Maqaasid* that it is not authentic, and he quotes the saying of Ibnul-Qayyim about it: "It was a saying of the idol-worshippers who used to think good of stones." And refer to my aforementioned book (no.450).

22. Soorah Al-Baqarah (2): 275

So both trade and usury are from the 'natural means' to attain wealth. However Allaah, the Most High, permitted the first and forbade the second.

HOW ARE WE TO KNOW THE CORRECTNESS OF A MEANS, AND THAT IT IS LAWFUL AND PRESCRIBED IN THE *SHAREE'AH*?

The correct way to know whether natural means (*al-wasaailul-Kawniyyah*) and means to attain *Sharee'ah* goals (*al-wasaailush-Shar'iyyah*) are prescribed is to refer back to the Book and the *Sunnah*, and to carefully check and confirm what is reported about them, and to examine the meaning and indication of relevant texts. There is no other way whatsoever.

For the permissibility of using a particular 'natural means' there are two conditions: Firstly that it is something lawful in the *Sharee'ah*, and secondly: that it is confirmed that it actually attains the goal, or that it is likely to do so.

As for the means prescribed for *Sharee'ah* goals then the only condition for them is that they are established in the *Sharee'ah*, this and nothing else.

So the use of the small animal, in the example which we mentioned previously, as an alleged means to gain knowledge of hidden and unseen affairs, is from the angle of 'natural means' futile and false, being demolished by experience and consideration. Then from the angle of *Sharee'ah* means, it is Unbelief and misguidance. Allaah has clearly explained its futility and has warned against it. Unfortunately people very often confuse these matters and think that by merely establishing that a certain means is beneficial then that shows that it is permissible and prescribed in the *Sharee'ah*. It may occur that one of them calls upon a deceased righteous person loved by Allaah (*walee*), or call for the assistance of a deceased person. Then he finds that what he called for comes about, and he attains what he desired. Then he claims that this is a proof of the ability of the dead and the pious occupants of the graves to come to peoples aid, and that it is permissible to supplicate to them and to ask them for assistance. Their only evidence for this is that they attained what they desired. We have read, unfortunately, many examples like this in books written about the religion. The author will say, or quote someone else as saying, for example, that he was in great distress and so called upon a certain *walee*, or a certain pious person, calling upon him by name, and that he then appeared in person or came in a dream and helped him and brought about what he desired. This poor person and his like do not realise that even if this had actually occurred, that it was only something done by Allaah, the Mighty and Majestic, as a means of allowing the idolaters and the innovators to go further astray in their misguidance, and as a trial for them, and as part of His plan against them, as a fitting reward for their turning away from the Book and the *Sunnah*, and for their following their desires and their devils.

So the person who says those words is allowing people to supplicate and call for aid upon others besides Allaah, the Most High, whereas such a call for aid (*istighaathah*) is nothing but Major *Shirk*. He allows this just because of something which happened with him or with someone else and it may even be that this story was fabricated and invented in the first place or has been distorted and exaggerated to misguide people. It is also possible that it was a true event, and that he erred in his judgement about the one who was saved and the one who gave the assistance. He thought that he was a pious person loved by Allaah whereas actually he was an accursed devil who did that with a wicked intention which was to fool and misguide the people, and to cause them to fall into Unbelief and misguidance knowingly or unknowingly. Indeed there are many reports about the idol-worshippers in the days of ignorance that they used to go to an idol and call upon it and then think that the one who was speaking to them and replying to them was the idol whom they worshipped besides Allaah. In reality it was none but an accursed devil who wished to misguide them and drown them in false beliefs.

So what is important here is that we realise that experience or reports of occurrences are not correct means of establishing that religious actions are actually correct and prescribed in the *Sharee'ah*. Rather the sole acceptable means to know that, is to establish the judgement of the *Sharee'ah* about it, and that is to be found in the Book and the *Sunnah*, nothing else. The most important area where people become confused here is what relates to the world of the Hidden and the Unseen (*al-Ghayb*)[23] and their seeking access to it by one means or another, such as going to fortune-tellers, palm-readers, astrologers, sorcerers and witches. You find that they believe that these people have knowledge of the Hidden and the Unseen since they are able to inform them about some things which are hidden from them. Then things sometimes occur as narrated by these people, so they therefore think that this is something permissible and allowed. Their evidence is that what these people told of actually occurred. This is a grave error and clear misguidance, since the mere fact that benefit is attained through a particular means is not enough to establish that this means is lawful and prescribed in the *Sharee'ah*. For example selling wine may lead to benefit for its owner and may lead to his becoming rich and wealthy, likewise gambling and lotteries sometimes, and because of this our Lord, the Blessed and the Most High, said about them:

$$يَسۡـَٔلُونَكَ عَنِ ٱلۡخَمۡرِ وَٱلۡمَيۡسِرِۖ قُلۡ فِيهِمَآ إِثۡمٞ كَبِيرٞ وَمَنَٰفِعُ لِلنَّاسِ وَإِثۡمُهُمَآ أَكۡبَرُ مِن نَّفۡعِهِمَاۗ وَيَسۡـَٔلُونَكَ مَاذَا يُنفِقُونَ قُلِ ٱلۡعَفۡوَۗ كَذَٰلِكَ يُبَيِّنُ ٱللَّهُ لَكُمُ ٱلۡأٓيَٰتِ لَعَلَّكُمۡ تَتَفَكَّرُونَ ۝$$

" **They ask you (O Muhammad (ﷺ)) concerning alcoholic drink and gambling. Say: "In them is a great sin, and (some) benefit for men, but the sin of them is**

---

23. Translator's note: i.e. matters relating to Allaah, His Angels, Predecree, Paradise and the Fire and so on, which we can only know about through the Revelation brought by the Messenger of Allaah (ﷺ). Whenever the words 'The Unseen' or 'The Hidden and the Unseen' occur in this book this is what is meant.

greater than their benefit."[24]

Yet despite this they are both forbidden (*haraam*), and the ten people connected with the alcoholic drinks are cursed, as occurs in the *hadeeth*.[25]

Going to fortune-tellers is likewise forbidden since its prohibition in the religion is established and a warning against it. The Prophet (ﷺ) said: *Whoever goes to a fortune-teller, and believes what he says then he has nothing to do with what was sent down upon Muhammad.*[26]

He (ﷺ) said: *Whoever goes to a diviner*[27] *and asks him about anything, then Prayer will not be accepted from him for forty nights.*[28]

Also Mu'aawiyah ibn al-Haakim al-Sulamee said to the Prophet (ﷺ): "Amongst us there are people who go to the fortune-tellers." So he (ﷺ) said: *Do not go to fortune-tellers.*[29]

The noble Messenger (ﷺ) explained how it is that the fortune-tellers and the sorcerers are able to obtain information about some unseen matters. He (ﷺ) said: *When Allaah has decreed a matter from above the heavens the angels*

---

24. Soorah Al-Baqarah (2): 219

25. Translator's note: Ibn 'Umar reports that Allaah's Messenger(ﷺ) said: *Allaah has cursed alcoholic drinks, he who drinks them, he who pours them, he who*
sells them, he who buys them, he who produces them, he who asks for them to be produced, he who conveys them, he who requests that they be conveyed, and he who devours their price. [*Saheeh*: Reported by Aboo Daawood (translation 4/1042/no.3666) and al-Haakim (2/32): *saheehul-Jaami'* (no.5091).

26. Reported by Ahmad and Aboo Daawood (translation 3/1095/no.3985) and its chain of narration is *Saheeh* (authentic).

27. Translator's note: Those who claim knowledge of the Unseen and claim to be able to discover things which have been lost.

28. Reported by Muslim (translation 4/1211/no.5540).

29. Reported by Muslim (translation 4/1209/no.5532) and others.

beat their wings in submission to His Saying which sounds like chains being dragged over smooth rock. Then when fear is removed from their hearts they say: 'What has your Lord said?' They say: 'The truth and He is the Most High, the Most Great. Then those who listen by stealth [i.e. devils] hear that, and those who listen by stealth are one above the other like this... (and Sufyaan, one of the narrators of the *hadeeth*, and he is (Sufyaan) ibn 'Uyainah as al-Haafidh Ibn Katheer points out in his *Tafseer* (3/537), indicated with his hand, spreading the fingers of his right hand and placing one over the other.) *... so a flame may overtake and burn the one listening by stealth before he passes it on to the next, and it may not reach him until he has transmitted it to the one below him until it is passed down to the earth, (or probably Sufyaan said: "Until the news reaches the earth.") Then it is placed in the mouth of the sorcerer who will add a hundred lies to it. So he will be true in that one, so the people will say: 'Did he not tell us that on such and such day such and such would occur, and we have found it to be true? (with regard to the news which came down from the heavens.)*[30]

The like of this is also reported in another *hadeeth* from Ibn 'Abbaas, *radiyallaahu 'anhumaa*, who said: "Allaah's Messenger (ﷺ) was sitting with a group of his companions when the light of a star shone. So he (ﷺ) said: *What had you used to say in the days of ignorance?* They said: We used to say: 'That it indicated the birth or death of a great man.' So Allaah's Messenger (ﷺ) said: *Rather they are not flung for the death nor the birth of anyone. Rather our Lord, the Blessed and the Most High, when He decrees a matter then the bearers of the Throne declare His glory and freedom from all imperfections. Then the occupants of the heavens next to them declare His glory and freedom from all imperfections, until their declarations of His glory and perfection reach the lowest heaven. Then the inhabitants of the heaven below the bearers of the Throne ask the bearers of the Throne: 'What did your Lord say?' So*

---

30. Reported by al-Bukhaaree in a number of places (translation 6/187/no.223 and 6/306/no.324).

they inform them and the inhabitants of each heaven inform those of the next, until the news reaches the heaven of this world and the Jinn seek to overhear and have (meteors) flung at them. So whatever they convey as it is then it is true, however they adulterate it with lies and add to it."[31]

So from these two *hadeeth* and others we know that a link between humans and *Jinns* occurs, and that the *Jinn* informs the fortune-teller of some true reports to which the fortune-teller adds other false reports which he concocts and then he narrates this to the people. They therefore find some to be true. However despite this, the Wise Law-Giver forbade going to these fortune-tellers, and warned against believing what they say, as has just preceded.

At this point it should not escape us that the fortune-tellers, diviners and astrologers have continued to have a great influence upon many people, even in this time which people claim to be the age of knowledge and enlighten-ment, and of civilisation and culture. They think that the time of fortune-tellers, sorcerers and magicians and their influence has ceased and passed away. However one who investigates carefully and looks at reports of such things from here and there will know for certain that they still have a hold over many people, except that they have distinguished themselves and taken on modern day disguises, which are not noticed except by a few. So the phe-nomenon of spiritualists causing spirits to appear and speaking with them, and getting in touch with them by various means is nothing but a form of this new branch of sorcery and fortune-telling by which people are lead astray and taken away from their religion to be attached instead to false and futile delusions. They consider these things to be knowledge and from the religion, whereas in reality knowledge and the religion are free and far removed from them. So in conclusion it is not permissible to affirm 'natural means', nor what is thought to be a means to the *Sharee'ah* goal, nor to use such means until it has been

---

31. Reported by Ahmad (1/218), Muslim (translation 4/1210/no.5538), at-Tirmidhee (9/91:*at-Tuhfah*) and others.

established that it is indeed something permitted in the *Sharee'ah*. Then with regard to 'natural means' it is also necessary to establish that they are valid/functional and beneficial, through observation and experience.

A further point that must be noted is that when it is established that something is a valid 'natural means', then if there is no prohibition of it in the *Sharee'ah*, then that is enough to make it permissible and usable. In this regard the scholars say: "The basic principle about things (worldly or non-shar'ee) is that they are permissible." But as for the means to attain *Sharee'ah* goals, then the mere fact that the Wise Law-Giver has not directly forbidden them is not sufficient to make it permissible to use them, as many people mistakenly think. Rather there must be an established *Sharee'ah* text which allows and recommends them. This is because a recommendation is more than a mere allowance, since it (a recommended action) is something which draws one closer to Allaah, the Most High, and such things cannot be established by the mere fact that no prohibition of them is reported. Concerning this one of the *Salaf* (Pious Predecessors) said: "Every form of worship which was not something done by the Companions of Allaah's Messenger(ﷺ), then do not do it." This is taken from the *ahaadeeth* forbidding innovating in the religion, and they are well-known. Therefore Shaykhul-Islaam Ibn Taymiyyah, *rahimahullaah*, said: "The basic principle with regard to worship is that all actions are forbidden and with regard to worldly affairs that all actions are permissible, unless there is a text." So remember this since it is very important and will help you to see the truth in matters about which the people disagree.

c h a p t e r   T H R E E

Lawful and Prescribed *Tawassul* and its types

From what has preceded we know that there are two separate matters, the first of which is that the use of a means (*tawassul*) must be prescribed, and that this can only be known through an authentic proof from the Book and the Sunnah. The second matter is that the *tawassul* should be by means of a correct natural means by which one does indeed reach what is desired.

We know that Allaah, the Mighty and Majestic, ordered us to supplicate to Him and to call upon Him for aid. He says:

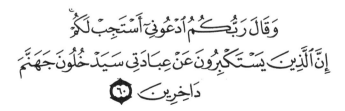

"And your Lord said: "Invoke Me (and ask Me for anything) I will respond to your (invocation). Verily! Those

who scorn My worship they will surely enter Hell in humiliation!"[32]

He, the Most High, says:

$$وَإِذَا سَأَلَكَ$$

$$عِبَادِى عَنِّى فَإِنِّى قَرِيبٌ أُجِيبُ دَعْوَةَ ٱلدَّاعِ إِذَا دَعَانِ فَلْيَسْتَجِيبُوا لِى وَلْيُؤْمِنُوا بِى لَعَلَّهُمْ يَرْشُدُونَ ﴿١٨٦﴾$$

"And when My slaves ask you (O Muhammad (ﷺ)) concerning Me, then (answer them), I am indeed near to them (by My Knowledge). I respond to the invocations of the supplicant when he calls on Me (without any mediator or intercessor). So let them obey Me and believe in Me, so that they may be led aright."[33]

He, the Mighty, has prescribed for us a number of types of prescribed means (*tawassul*) which are beneficial and reach the desired goal. Allaah has granted that He will certainly respond to those who call upon Him by these means, as long as the other conditions for acceptability of the supplication are fulfilled. So now let us look, without clinging blindly to one opinion or prejudice, at what is apparent after careful research, of what is reported in the Noble Book and the pure *Sunnah*, and that is that there are three types of *Tawassul* which Allaah, the Most High, has prescribed and encouraged. Some of them are reported in the *Qur'aan* and were used by the Messenger (ﷺ) and he encouraged their use. Amongst them there is not to be found any *tawassul* by

---

32. Soorah Ghaafir (40): 60
33. Soorah Al-Baqarah (2): 186

means of any person, nor their status, nor their rights, nor their station. So this shows that this is not prescribed and does not enter into the general *'waseelah'* which is mentioned in the two *Aayaat*. As for the types of prescribed *tawassul* which are indicated then they are:

I.   *TAWASSUL* (SEEKING A MEANS OF NEARNESS) TO ALLAAH, THE MOST HIGH, BY MEANS OF HIS PERFECT AND MOST BEAUTIFUL NAMES OR HIS EXALTED ATTRIBUTES.

Such as the Muslim saying in his supplication: "O Allaah I ask You by Your being the Most Merciful, the Bestower of Mercy, the Most Gracious Knower of all that is hidden, the Fully-acquainted: that You grant me safety and well-being." (*Allaahumma innee Asaluka biannaka Anta ar-Rahmanur-Raheem...*). Or such as: "O Allaah I ask you, by Your Mercy which comprehends everything, that You have mercy upon me and forgive me... ." Like it is the saying of a person: "O Allaah I ask You by Your love for Muhammad... ," since love is one of His Attributes. The proof for the prescription of this form of *tawassul* is the Saying of Allaah, the Mighty and Majestic:

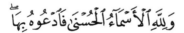

"And (all) the Most Beautiful Names belong to Allaah, so call on Him by them."[34]

The meaning of this is: Call upon Allaah, the Most High, by means of (performing *tawassul* with) His perfect Names, and there is no doubt that His exalted Attributes fit into this since His Names are Attributes of His.

From this is what Allaah, the Most High, mentions about the supplication of Sulaymaan, *'alaihis-salaam*, when he said:

---

34. Soorah Al-A'raaf (7): 180

$$وَقَالَ رَبِّ أَوْزِعْنِيٓ أَنْ أَشْكُرَ
نِعْمَتَكَ ٱلَّتِيٓ أَنْعَمْتَ عَلَيَّ وَعَلَىٰ وَٰلِدَيَّ وَأَنْ أَعْمَلَ صَٰلِحًا
تَرْضَىٰهُ وَأَدْخِلْنِي بِرَحْمَتِكَ فِي عِبَادِكَ ٱلصَّٰلِحِينَ ﴿١٩﴾$$

"He said: "My Lord! Inspire and bestow upon me the power and ability that I may be grateful for Your Favours which You have bestowed on me and on my parents, and that I may do righteous good deeds that will please You, and admit me by Your Mercy among Your righteous slaves."[35]

Also from the proofs of this is the saying of the Prophet(ﷺ) in an established supplication which he would say before giving the *Salaam* in his Prayer: *O Allaah by Your Knowledge of the Hidden and Unseen, and Your Power over the creation, grant me life for as long as You know that life is good for me, and grant me death when death is good for me...*[36] From them is that he (ﷺ) heard a man saying in his *tashahhud*: "O Allaah, I ask You, O Allaah, the One, the Single, the Self Sufficient Master Who needs none, but all have need of (Him), Who does not beget, nor was He begotten, nor is there any like Him..., that You forgive me my sins, indeed You are the Most forgiving, the Most Merciful." So he (ﷺ) said: *He has been forgiven, he has been forgiven.*[37]

The Prophet (ﷺ) also heard another man saying in his *tashahhud*: "O Allaah

---

35. Soorah An-Naml (27): 19

36. Reported by an-Nasaa'ee, al-Haakim and he declared it *saheeh* and adh-Dhahabee agreed with him and it is as they said.

37. Reported by Aboo Daawood, an-Nasaa'ee, Ahmad and others its *isnaad* (chain of narration) is *saheeh*.

I ask You by virtue of the fact that all praise belongs to You, none has the right to be worshipped but You, alone, having no partner. The Great Bestower of all blessings, O Originator of the heavens and the earth, O Possessor of Majesty and Honour, O Ever-Living, O Sustainer and Protector of all that exists. Indeed I ask You for Paradise and I seek Your refuge from the Fire." So the Prophet(ﷺ) said to his Companions: *Do you know what he has supplicated with?* They said: 'Allaah and His Messenger know best.' He said: *By Him in Whose Hand is my soul he has supplicated to Allaah by His Great name* (and in a narration: *by His greatest name*) *if He is called upon by it then He responds and if He is asked by it He gives.*[38]

From this is his (ﷺ) saying: *Whoever is greatly troubled and says: "O Allaah I am Your slave, son of Your male slave and female slave. My forelock is in Your Hand. Your judgement is continually operative upon me. Your sentence concerning me is just. I ask You by every name which is Yours, with which You named Yourself, taught to anyone from Your creation, or sent down in Your Book, or which You kept to Yourself in the knowledge of the Hidden with You, that You make the Qur'aan the spring of my heart, the light of my chest, the removal of my sadness and of my anxiety" then Allaah will remove his anxiety and sorrow and replace it with joy.*[39]

Also from this is what is reported from his (ﷺ) seeking Allaah's refuge with the words: *O Allaah, I seek refuge in Your Might, none has the right to be worshipped but You, ...*[40]

Also from them is what Anas, *radiyallaahu 'anhu* reports about the Prophet (ﷺ), that when a matter grieved the Prophet, he would say: *O Ever-Living, O*

---

38. Reported by Aboo Daawood, an-Nasaa'ee and Ahmad and others with *saheeh isnaad*.

39. Reported by Ahmad (no.3712) and the wording is his, and al-Haakim (1/509) and others and its *isnaad* is *saheeh* as I have explained in *as-Saheehah* (no.199).

40. Al-Bukhaaree and Muslim.

Sustainer and Protector of all that exists, by Your Mercy I beg for Your aid.[41]

So these *ahaadeeth* and their like show the prescription of *tawassul* to Allaah, the Most High, with one of His Names or His Attributes, and that this is something which Allaah loves and is pleased with. Therefore it was done by Allaah's Messenger (ﷺ) and Allaah, the Blessed and Most High, says:

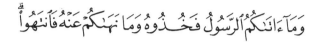

"**And whatsoever the Messenger (Muhammad (ﷺ)) gives you, take it, and whatsoever he forbids you, abstain (from it).**"[42]

So it is prescribed for us to call upon Allaah, the one free of all imperfections, in the manner which His Messenger (ﷺ) called upon Him. That is a thousand times better than calling upon Him with supplications which we originate and in forms which we ourselves invent.

II.   *TAWASSUL* TO ALLAAH, THE MOST HIGH, BY MEANS OF A RIGHTEOUS DEED WHICH THE PERSON SUPPLICATING HAS DONE.

Such as the Muslim's saying: "O Allaah by my *Eemaan* in You, and my love for You, and my following of Your Messenger, forgive me..." or his saying: "O Allaah I ask You by my love for Muhammad (ﷺ) and my *Eemaan* in him, that you rescue me..." From it is that the person supplicated and mentions an important pious act which he has done, and in which he feared Allaah, the One free of all imperfections, and did in obedience to Him, hoping for His reward and fearing His punishment, and giving precedence to pleasing Him and obey-

---

41. Reported by at-Tirmidhee (1/267: '*at-Tuhfah*') and al-Haakim (1/509) and it is a *hasan hadeeth*.

42. Soorah Al-Hashr (59): 7

ing Him over everything else, and then using that as a means of *tawassul* in his supplication, so that it is more liable to be accepted and responded to.

This form of *tawassul* is good and beautiful and has been prescribed by Allaah, the Most High, and it is pleasing to Him. Its prescription is shown by the Saying of Allaah, the Most High:

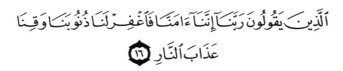

"Those who say: "Our Lord! We have indeed believed, so forgive us our sins and save us from the punishment of the Fire."[43]

His Saying:

رَّبَّنَآ ءَامَنَّا بِمَآ أَنزَلْتَ وَٱتَّبَعْنَا ٱلرَّسُولَ فَٱكْتُبْنَا مَعَ ٱلشَّٰهِدِينَ ۝

"Our Lord! We believe in what You have sent down, and we follow the Messenger (Jesus); so write us down among those who bear witness (to the truth i.e. none has the right to be worshipped except Allaah)."[44]

_____

43. Soorah Aali-'Imraan (3): 6
44. Soorah Aali-'Imraan (3): 53

29

His Saying:

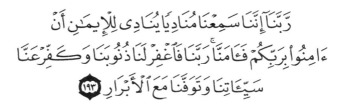

"Our Lord! Verily, we have heard the call of one
(Muhammad (ﷺ)) calling to Faith: 'Believe in your
Lord,' and we have believed. Our Lord! Forgive us our
sins and remit from us our evil deeds, and make us die
in the state of righteousness along with *Al-Abraar*
(those who are obedient to Allaah and strictly follow His
Orders)."[45]

and His Saying:

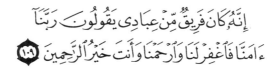

"Verily! There was a party of My Slaves, who used to say:
"Our Lord! We believe, so forgive us, and have mercy on
us, for You are the Best of all who show mercy!"[46]

This form of *tawassul* is also proven by what Buraidah ibn al-Husayb, *radiyallaahu 'anhu* reports, saying: "The Prophet (ﷺ) heard a man saying: 'O Allaah

---

45. Soorah Aali-'Imraan (3): 193.

46. Soorah Al-Muminoon (23): 109

I ask You by virtue of the fact that I testify that You are Allaah, none but You has the right to be worshipped. The One, The Self-Sufficient Master whom all creatures have need of. He who does not beget, nor was He begotten, Who has no equal or anything comparable to Him.' So he (ﷺ) said: *He has asked Allaah by His greatest name, which if He is asked by it He gives and if He is supplicated to with it, He responds.*"[47]

Also from this is what occurs in the story of the companions of the cave, as is reported by 'Abdullaah ibn 'Umar, *radiyallaahu 'anhumaa*, who said: I heard Allaah's Messenger (ﷺ) say: *Three men, amongst those who came before you set out until night came and they reached a cave, so they entered it. But a boulder rolled down from the mountain and blocked the entrance of the cave. So they said: Nothing can rescue you from this rock except that you sup-plicate to Allaah by mentioning righteous deeds you have done. (and in the narration of Muslim: So one of them said to the others: Think of righteous deeds which you have done purely for Allaah by making mention of them, that He might release you). So one of them said: 'O Allaah I had two elderly parents and I had not used to give precedence over them to my family and slaves in giving them milk to drink. But one day I was delayed in seeking after something (in the narration of Muslim: for fodder) and I did not return with the flock until they (my parents) had slept. So I milked the animals for them but found that they were both asleep. However I hated to give milk to my family and slaves before them, so I waited with the bowl in my hand for them to awake. Then with the break of dawn they awoke and drank their milk. O Allaah if I did that seeking Your Face, then relieve us from this situa-tion caused by the rock.' So it moved slightly, but they were unable to escape.* The Prophet (ﷺ) said: *The next said: 'O Allaah my uncle had a daughter and she was the most beloved of the people to me and I tried to persuade her to have sexual relations with me, but she refused me until she suffered from*

---

47. Reported by Ahmad (5/349/350), Aboo Daawood (translation 1/389/no.1488) and others and its *isnaad* is *saheeh*.

a year of famine. Then she came to me and I gave her a hundred and twen-
ty deenars on the condition that she would comply with my desire for her, so
she agreed. But when I was about to fulfil my desire she said: 'It is unlawful
for you to break (in a narration of Muslim: O servant of Allaah, fear Allaah
and do not break) the seal except by lawful means. So I felt ashamed to com-
mit the crime against her so I left her alone, and she was the most dear of all
the people to me, and I (also) left the gold which I had given her. O Allaah if
I did that seeking Your Face then release us from the situation we are in.' So
the rock opened further but they were still unable to escape. The Prophet
(ﷺ) said: *And the third said: 'O Allaah I employed some labourers and paid*
them their wages except a single man who did not take his wages and went
away. I invested his wages and it grew into a great deal of property. Then
after some time he came to me and said: 'O servant of Allaah, give me my
wages.' So I said to him: 'All the camels, cows, sheep and slaves that you see
are your wages.' So he said: 'O servant of Allaah, do not mock me.' So I said:
'I am not mocking you.' So he took all of that and led them away and did not
leave any of it. O Allaah if I did that seeking Your Face, then release us from
our situation.' So the rock moved and they walked out of the cave.[48]

So it is clear from this *hadeeth* that when these three Believers were in distress
and in such difficulty, and when they despaired of any means of escape except
that Allaah, the Blessed and Most High, alone should save them, then they
turned to Him and supplicated purely and sincerely to Him. They also mentioned righteous actions which they had done being aware of Allaah in times
of ease, hoping that their Lord would in return now rescue them in their time
of hardship. Just as is reported in the *hadeeth* of the Prophet (ﷺ) in which
there occurs: ... *Remember Allaah in times of ease and He will remember you*
in times of difficulty.[49]

---

48. Reported by al-Bukhaaree (3/260/no.472) and the wording is his and Muslim
(4/1432/no.6607) and an-Nasaa'ee and others.

49. Reported by Ahmad from Ibn 'Abbaas, and its chain of narration is *saheeh* (authentic) due
to supports, as I have explained in *Zilaalil-Jannah fee takhreejis-Sunnah* (no.138).

So they sought a means of nearness (*tawassul*) to Him, the One free of all imperfections, through those actions. So the first used his kindness to his parents as *tawassul* and his merciful and compassionate treatment of them to the point that it lead him to that singular and beautiful action, and I do not think any other person, except for the Prophets, would reach this level of kindness and goodness to their parents.

Then the second used as *tawassul* his abstention from fornicating with his uncle's daughter, and he had the strongest desire for her and she was at his disposal and had submitted to Him unwillingly due to hunger and need. But she reminded him of Allaah, the Mighty and Majestic, and his heart accepted the admonition and his limbs trembled and he left her and the money which he had given to her.

Then the third used as *tawassul* his preserving the right of his employee, who left his wages which amounted to a measure of rice, as occurs in an authentic narration of the *hadeeth*, and went off. So the employer invested this until it grew to amount to sheep, cows, camels and slaves. Then when the employee was later in need of his wages, he requested his meagre earnings from the man who employed him. He in turn handed over all the wealth which astonished the worker and caused him to think that he was being mocked. However when it was clear that the man was serious and that this was all the product of his wages he led them off with joy and wonder, not leaving anything behind. Indeed, by Allaah, the action of the employer here reached an astonishing level of beneficent treatment of the worker and was an exemplary example of fine and honourable treatment of those whom one is in charge of. It was of such a level that the position of all those who claim to support the workers and the common man does not even reach a hundredth of it, those who make a profitable business out of their claims to protect the rights of the poor and needy, and to treat them fairly and give them their rights. So the supplication of these three to their Lord, the One free of all imperfections, using as a means of nearness to Him these extremely righteous and noble actions, declaring that they had done them purely and solely to seek the pleasure of Allaah, the Most High, not intending by them any worldly or personal benefit or any wealth. So they hoped that Allaah, the Majestic would release them from their difficulty and free them from their trial, so He, the One free of all imperfections responded to their supplication, relieved their distress and did as they had hoped of Him by granting them a clear miracle, causing the rock to move away in three stages each time one of them supplicated so that it opened totally when the third man finished his supplication, after their having been in a state where death was imminent. Then our noble Messenger (ﷺ) narrated this fine story to us after it was something unknown and hidden, known only to Allaah, the One free of all imperfections and the Most High. He informed us of this to remind us of excellent and exemplary actions performed by excellent and exemplary followers of the previous prophets in order that we should follow their example, act as they acted, and draw valuable lessons and admonition from their story. It cannot be said: 'These actions were done before the sending of our Prophet Muhammad (ﷺ) and so do not apply to us,' based upon what is the correct view in the Principles of *Fiqh* that prescribed laws for those who came before us are not prescribed laws for us. This is not said here because the Prophet (ﷺ) quoted this event in terms of praise and esteem, and this was a tacit approval of it from the Prophet (ﷺ). Indeed it is even more than a tacit approval of their righteous actions: it is not except an explanation of and a practical example of how the previous *Aayaat* are to be put into practice. The revealed laws agree in their teaching's and guidance and this is not surprising since they come from a single source and emanate from a single light, particularly with regard the condition of people and their relation to their Lord, the One free of all imperfections, so they only differ very slightly and very rarely as required by the wisdom of Allaah, the One free of all imperfections.

III. SEEKING A MEANS OF NEARNESS TO ALLAAH, THE MOST HIGH, BY
THE SUPPLICATION OF A RIGHTEOUS MAN.

If a Muslim falls into great difficulty or a great misfortune befalls him, and he
knows that he has been very negligent with regard to Allaah, the Blessed and
Most High's, rights upon him, so he wishes to use a strong means of drawing
nearer to Allaah. So he goes to man whom he believes to be righteous and to
be one who fears Allaah, or a person possessing excellence and knowledge of
the Book and the *Sunnah*, and he asks him to supplicate to his Lord for him
that He (i.e. Allaah) should relieve his distress and remove what had befallen
him. This is a further type of prescribed *tawassul* which is proven and guided
to in the pure *Sharee'ah*. Examples of it are found in the noble *Sunnah* and
examples of it are found in the practice of the noble Companions, may Allaah
the Most High be pleased with them all. Anas ibn Maalik, *radiyallaahu 'anhu*
reports, saying: "The people were afflicted with drought in the time of the
Prophet (ﷺ), so whilst the Prophet (ﷺ) was giving the *khutbah* [upon the
minbar], standing, on the day of *Jumu'ah* a bedouin stood [and in a narration:
entered] [from the people of the desert] [through a door which faced the *minbar*] [near to the house sold for the repayment of a debt[50], and Allaah's
Messenger (ﷺ) was standing. So he stood facing Allaah's Messenger (ﷺ)]
and said: "O Messenger of Allaah, the livestock are dying and the children are
hungry [and in a narration: destroyed] [and in another narration: the horses
are dying and the sheep are dying] [and in another wording: the cattle are
dying and the roads are cut off] so supplicate to Allaah for us [that he should
give us rain] [and in another: that he should give us a downpour]." So he
raised up his hands and supplicated [until I saw the whiteness of his armpits]:
[*O Allaah bless us with rain, O Allaah bless us with rain*] [and the people
raised up their hands along with him supplicating] [and he did not mention
that he turned his cloak inside out, nor that he faced the *Qiblah*], and [By
Allaah] we could not see [any clouds nor] any trace of clouds [nor anything,

---

50. *Daarul-Qadaa* - a house which belonged to 'Umar ibn al-Khattaab and which was sold in
order to repay a debt.

and there was no building or house between us and sal'[51] [and in a narration: Anas said: And the sky was clear as glass] [He said: So I then saw a large cloud like a shield and when it came to the middle of the sky it spread and it rained]. By Him in Whose Hand is my soul, as soon as he had lowered his hands clouds like mountains had gathered, and he did not descend from the *minbar* until I saw the rain dripping from his beard, [and in a narration: suddenly the wind blew gathering clouds which came together and then rain poured down from the sky] [and he came down from the *minbar* and prayed the Prayer] [so we went out and waded through the water until we reached our homes] [and in a narration: and it was such that a person could hardly reach his home]. So it continued to rain that day, and the next, and the next, and that which followed, until the following *Jumu'ah* and it had not ceased [so the waterways of al-Madeenaah were filled] [and in a narration: so, by Allaah we did not see the sun for a week]. Then that bedouin or someone else stood up [and in a narration: Then a man entered from that door in the next *Jumu'ah* and Allaah's Messenger (ﷺ) was standing giving *khutbah*, so he stood facing him] and he said: O Messenger of Allaah, buildings are being destroyed, [and in a narration: houses are collapsing, roads are cut off and the cattle are dying] [and in a narration: the traveller cannot proceed and the roads are blocked] and livestock are being drowned. So supplicate to Allaah [to withhold it] for us [so the Prophet (ﷺ) smiled] and he raised his hands and said: *O Allaah, around us and not upon us, [O Allaah upon the tops of mountains, hillocks [and hills] and river beds and places where trees grow]*. So he did not point with his hand in any direction except that the clouds cleared away producing a clear circular hole [and in a narration: so I looked and saw the clouds separating around al-Madeenah [to the right and the left] forming [a sort of crown] [and in another: so the clouds cleared away from al-Madeenah just as clothes are removed] and it was now raining all around us, but not raining upon us at all [in a narration: not a drop] [and we went out walking in the sunshine]. So Allaah showed them a miracle for His Prophet (ﷺ) and His response to his

---

51. A small mountain in al-Madeenah.

supplication. The valley of Qanaat was flooded for a month, and no one came from outside except that he told of abundant rain."[52]

Anas ibn Maalik, *radiyallaahu 'anhu*[53] narrates from 'Umar ibn al-Khattaab, *radiyallaahu 'anhu*, that when the people suffered from drought he used to ask al-'Abbaas ibn al-Muttalib to pray for rain for them. He used to say: "O Allaah we used to request our Prophet (ﷺ) to supplicate to You for rain (*natawassalu ilaika*) and You would bless us with rain. Now we ask the uncle of our Prophet to supplicate to You (*natawassalu ilaika*), so grant us rain." What the saying of 'Umar (*Inaa kunnaa natawassalu ilaika binabiyyinaa wa inaa natawassalu ilaika bi'ammi nabiyyinaa*) means is: We used to go to our Prophet (ﷺ) and ask him to supplicate for us, and draw nearer to Allaah by means of his supplicating for us, and now that he (ﷺ) has passed on to the company of the highest Angels and it is not now possible for him to supplicate for us, then now we go to the uncle of our Prophet (ﷺ), al-'Abbaas, and ask him to supplicate for us. It certainly does not mean that they used to supplicate saying: 'O Allaah, by the status of Your Prophet grant us rain' and then after his (ﷺ) death say: 'O Allaah by the status of al-'Abbaas grant us rain', since this supplication is an innovation having no proof or basis in the Book or the *Sunnah*, and it was not done by a single one of the Pious Predecessors, may Allaah the Most High be pleased with them all, as will be discussed in more detail shortly, if Allaah wills.

---

52. Reported by al-Bukhaaree (transl: vol.2 [p.26,no.55] [p.67-72,nos.126-132], [p.73,no.134] [p.77,ch.20], [p.79,no.143]; vol.4, [p.504,no.782]; vol.8 [p.74,no.115]. I bring this in my abridgement of *Saheehul-Bukhaaree* (1/224-226,no.497) gathering its various narrations together, and this abridgement is being published in stages... I hope that Allaah, the Most High, will facilitate the publication of the rest, and hasten that since it contains many valuable points of benefit which a student of knowledge or one desiring knowledge of *Fiqh* cannot dispense with.

53. Reported by al-Bukhaaree (trans. 2/66/no.123 and 5/48/no.59) and Ibn Sa'd in *at-Tabaqaat* (4/28-29) and it is found in *Mukhtasarul-Bukhaaree* (no.536).

Also from this is what al-Haafidh Ibn 'Asaakir, *rahimahullaah ta'aalaa* reports in his *Tareekh* (18/151/1) with an authentic chain of narration[54] from the noble *tabi'ee* Sulaym ibn 'Aamir al-Khabaairee: "That the sky withheld any rain, so Mu'aawiyah ibn Abee Sufyaan and the people of Damascus went out to pray for rain. So when Mu'aawiyah sat upon the *minbar* he said: 'Where is Yazeed ibn al-Aswad al-Jurashee?' So the people called him and he came stepping between the people. Then Mu'aawiyah commanded him and he ascended the *minbar* and sat at his feet. Then Mu'aawiyah said: "O Allaah we are today asking the best and most noble amongst us to supplicate to You for us, O Allaah today we put Yazeed ibn al-Aswad al-Jurashee forward to supplicate to You for us," "O Yazeed raise up your hands to Allaah." So he raised up his hands and the people raised up their hands. Then very quickly rain-clouds like a large shield came quickly from the west, and the wind blew and it rained so profusely that people could hardly reach their houses."

Ibn 'Asaakir also reports with an authentic chain of narration that ad-Dahhaak ibn Qays went with the people to pray for rain, and he also said to Yazeed ibn al-Aswad: 'Stand up O he who weeps much!' and in a narration: "So he only supplicated three times before it rained so heavily that it almost drowned them."

So again we have Mu'aawiyah, *radiyallaahu 'anhu*, not doing *tawassul* by means of the Prophet (ﷺ) for the reason that has preceded, rather he used the supplication of that righteous man, Yazeed ibn al-Aswad, *rahimahullaah*, as a means of *tawassul*. So he asked him to supplicate to Allaah, the Most High, that He should bless them with rain. Then Allaah, the Blessed and the Most High, responded to his request, and the same thing occurred during the governership of al-Dahhaak ibn Qays.

---

54. Al-Haafidh al-'Asqalaanee also attributes it in *al-Isaabah* (3/634) to Aboo Zur'ah ad-Dimashqee and Ya'qoob ibn Sufyaan in his *Tareekh* with an authentic chain of narration from Sulaym ibn 'Aamir.

THE INCORRECTNESS AND FUTILITY OF SEEKING TO DO *TAWASSUL* IN ANY
WAY OTHER THAN THE THREE PRECEDING WAYS

So from what has preceded you know that prescribed *tawassul*, that which is
proven by the texts of the Book and the *Sunnah*, and which is proven by the
practice of the Pious Predecessors, and upon which there is consensus
(*ijmaa'*) of the Muslims is:

1. *Tawassul* by means of the Names of Allaah, the Blessed and
the Most High, and His Attributes.

2. *Tawassul* by means of a righteous action which the person
who is supplicating has done.

3. *Tawassul* by means of the supplication made by a righteous
man.

As for anything besides these types of *tawassul*, then there is disagreement
about it, and what we believe firmly and hold as our religion before Allaah, the
Most High, is that other ways are not permissible, and not prescribed. This is
because there is no acceptable proof for them, and these things have been spoken against by the verifying scholars in successive centuries of Islamic history.
Even though some of them have been allowed by some of the scholars, so [for
instance] Imaam Ahmad allowed *tawassul* by means of the Messenger (ﷺ)
alone, and others such as Imaam ash-Shawkaanee allowed *tawassul* by means
of him and other Prophets and the Pious. However we, as is the case in all matters where there is disagreement, follow whatever is supported by the proof
whatever that is, without blindly sticking to the opinions of men. We do not
align ourselves except with the truth. So with regard to the question of *tawassul*, which we are presently discussing, then we see that the truth is with those
who warn against *tawassul* by means of any created being, and we warn against
tawassul by means of any created being. Indeed they cannot find anything to
support what they hold except doubts which they raise and possibilities which

we will reply to shortly.

So we find many supplications in the Noble Qur'aan, and we do not find any of them containing any *tawassul* by means of the status, honour, right or position of any created being. Here are some of the noble supplications as examples. Our Lord, the Most Majestic, says, teaching us and guiding us how to supplicate:

لَا يُكَلِّفُ
ٱللَّهُ نَفْسًا إِلَّا وُسْعَهَا لَهَا مَا كَسَبَتْ وَعَلَيْهَا مَا ٱكْتَسَبَتْ
رَبَّنَا لَا تُؤَاخِذْنَا إِن نَّسِينَا أَوْ أَخْطَأْنَا رَبَّنَا وَلَا تَحْمِلْ
عَلَيْنَا إِصْرًا كَمَا حَمَلْتَهُ عَلَى ٱلَّذِينَ مِن قَبْلِنَا رَبَّنَا وَلَا
تُحَمِّلْنَا مَا لَا طَاقَةَ لَنَا بِهِۦ وَٱعْفُ عَنَّا وَٱغْفِرْ لَنَا وَٱرْحَمْنَا
أَنتَ مَوْلَىٰنَا فَٱنصُرْنَا عَلَى ٱلْقَوْمِ ٱلْكَٰفِرِينَ ﴿٢٨٦﴾

"Allaah burdens not a person beyond his scope. He gets reward for that (good) which he has earned, and he punished for that (evil) which he has earned. "Our Lord! Punish us not if we forget or fall into error, our Lord! Lay not on us a burden like that which You did lay on those before us (Jews and Christians); our Lord! Put not on us a burden greater than we have strength to bear. Pardon us and grant us Forgiveness. Have mercy on us. You are our *Maulaa* (Patron, supporter and protector, etc.) and give us victory over the disbelieving people."[55]

---

55. Soorah Al-Baqarah(2): 286

He says:

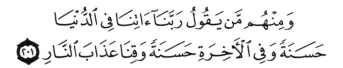

"And of them is he who says: 'Our Lord! Give us in this world that which is good and in the Hereafter that which is good, and save us from the torment of the Fire!'"[56]

He says:

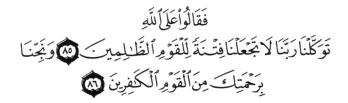

"They said: 'In Allaah we put our trust. Our Lord! Make us not a trial for the folk who are *dhaalimeen* (polytheists and wrong-doers). And save us by Your Mercy from the disbelieving folk.'"[57]

---

56. Soorah Al-Baqarah(2): 201
57. Soorah Yoonus (10): 85-86

41

He says:

وَإِذ

قَالَ إِبْرَٰهِيمُ رَبِّ اجْعَلْ هَٰذَا الْبَلَدَ ءَامِنًا وَاجْنُبْنِي وَبَنِيَّ أَن نَّعْبُدَ الْأَصْنَامَ ﴿٣٥﴾

رَبِّ اجْعَلْنِي مُقِيمَ الصَّلَوٰةِ وَمِن ذُرِّيَّتِي رَبَّنَا وَتَقَبَّلْ دُعَاءِ ﴿٤٠﴾ رَبَّنَا اغْفِرْ لِي وَلِوَٰلِدَيَّ وَلِلْمُؤْمِنِينَ يَوْمَ يَقُومُ الْحِسَابُ ﴿٤١﴾

"And (remember) when Ibraaheem said: 'O my Lord! Make this city (Makkah) one of peace and security, and keep me and my sons away from worshipping idols.' 'O my Lord! Make me one who offers prayers perfectly, and (also) from my offspring, our Lord! And accept my invocation.' 'Our Lord! Forgive me and my parents, and (all) the believers on the Day when the reckoning will be established.'"[58]

He says, upon the tongue of Moosaa, *'alaihis-salaam*:

قَالَ رَبِّ اشْرَحْ لِي صَدْرِي ﴿٢٥﴾

وَيَسِّرْ لِي أَمْرِي ﴿٢٦﴾ وَاحْلُلْ عُقْدَةً مِّن لِّسَانِي ﴿٢٧﴾

---

58. Soorah Ibraaheem (14): 35 & 40-41.

"(Moses) said: 'O my Lord! Open for me my chest (grant me self-confidence, contentment, and boldness). And ease my task for me; And make loose the knot (the defect) from my tongue, (i.e. remove the incorrectness from my speech).'"[59]

He, the One free of all imperfections, says:

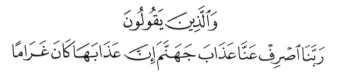

"And those who say: "Our Lord! Avert from us the torment of Hell. Verily! Its torment is ever an inseparable, permanent punishment."[60]

There are many other noble Qur'anic supplications, some of them are supplications which Allaah, the Most High, has taught us to call upon Him with, others are supplications which He relates to us from some of His prophets and messengers, or some of His worshippers and pious men whom He loves, and it is very clear that none of them contain any of that innovated *tawassul* which the blind-followers cling to and which the adversaries seek to argue for. Then if we look to the noble *Sunnah* to find the supplications which the Prophet (ﷺ) used to make and which Allaah was pleased with and taught him, and he in turn guided us to their excellence and beauty, then we find that they are in full conformity with the previous Qur'anic supplications, in that they are also free from any of the aforementioned innovated *tawassul*. So here are some of those Prophetic supplications: From them is the *Du'aaul-Istikhaarah* (Supplication requesting Allaah's help and guidance about a matter) which is

---

59. Soorah Taa Haa (20): 25-27
60. Soorah Al-Furqaan (25): 65

well-known and which the Prophet (ﷺ) used to teach his Companions, when one of them intended to carry something out, just as he would teach them the Qur'aan, and it is: *O Allaah I ask Your guidance through Your Knowledge, and I seek Your help through Your Power, and I ask You for Your great blessings. Indeed You are fully capable and I am not; You know and I do not, and You know whatever is Hidden and Unseen. O Allaah if You know that this matter is good for me in my religion, my worldly life and my Hereafter, and my present and future, then ordain it for me and make it easy for me, and bless me in it. If however You know that this matter is bad for me in my religion, my worldly life and my Hereafter, and my present and future, then keep it away from me, and turn me away from it, and ordain whatever is good for me wherever it is, then make me pleased with it.*[61]

Also from them is his supplication: *O Allaah set right for me my religion which is the safeguard of my affairs, and set right for me my worldly affairs wherein is my living, and set right for me my Hereafter which is the place of my after-life, and make life a source of increase in all good for me, and make death a rest for me from every evil.*[62]

O Allaah through Your knowledge of the Hidden and Unseen, and Your Power to create, grant me life for as long as You know that life is better for me, and take my soul when You know that death is better for me...[63]

O Allaah I ask You for right guidance, piety (taqwaa), chastity and contentment.[64]

---

61. Reported by al-Bukhaaree (translation 2/146/no.263) [See also *Authentic Supplications of the Prophet* by Waleed Al-Essa (no.123)].

62. Reported by Muslim (transl. 4/1425/6565).

63. Reported by an-Nasaa'ee with an authentic chain of narration, [*Authentic Supplications*, no.104].

64. Reported by Muslim (transl. 4/1425/no.6566).

O Allaah grant us such a share of fear of You as will prevent us from disobedience to You, and such obedience to You as will enable us to reach Your Paradise... [65]

O Allaah, Lord of Jibreel and Meekaaeel and Israafeel and Muhammad, we seek Your refuge from the Fire.[66]

There are very many supplications like this in the *Sunnah*, whereas we do not find a single authentic example of the innovated *tawassul* which is used by the adversaries.

What is certainly very strange is that you see these people turning away from the previous correct and prescribed types of *tawassul*. They hardly use anything from them in their supplications or when they are teaching the people, despite the fact that they are established in the Book, the *Sunnah* and the consensus of the *Ummah*. But instead of this you see them turning to supplications which they have invented and using forms of *tawassul* which they have innovated and which were not prescribed by Allaah, the Mighty and Majestic, nor were they used by His chosen Messenger (ﷺ), nor are they reported by the Pious Predecessors amongst this *Ummah*, the people of the three praiseworthy generations, and the best that can be said about their forms of tawassul is that they are things about which there is disagreement. So how deserving these people are of the Saying of Allaah, the Blessed and the Most High:

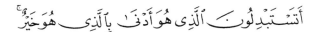

---

65. Reported by at-Tirmidhee who declared it *hasan* and it is as he said, [*Authentic Supplications* no.253].

66. Reported by al-Haakim and at-Tabaraanee with a chain of narration which is *hasan* due to supports as I have explained in *as-Saheehah* (no.1544).

"Would you exchange that which is better for that which is lower?"[67]

So perhaps this is one of the witnesses to the truth of what the noble *Tabi'ee* Hassaan ibn 'Atiyyah al-Muhaaribee, *rahimahullaah*, said: "No people introduce an innovation into their religion except that Allaah will take away a corresponding amount of their *Sunnah*, and will not restore it to them until the Day if Resurrection."[68]

We are not alone in criticising these innovated forms of *tawassul*, rather great imaams and scholars of the past preceded us in this criticism, and this is also confirmed in at least one of the schools of thought which people follow, and that is the *madhhab* of Aboo Haneefah, *rahimahullaah*. There occurs in *ad-Durrul-Mukhtaar* (2/630), and it is one of the most famous of the books of the Hanafees: "From Aboo Haneefah: It is not fitting at all that anyone should supplicate to Allaah except by Him, and using such supplications as have been permitted and ordered in the like of the Saying of Allaah, the Most High:

"And (all) the Most Beautiful Names belong to Allaah, so call upon Him by them."[69]

Its like is also found in *al-Fataawal-Hindiyyah* (5/280), and al-Qudooree[70] said in his large book of *Fiqh* called *Sharhul-Kharkhee* in the chapter of detested matters: "Bishr ibn al-Waleed said: Aboo Yoosuf narrated to us, that Aboo

---

67. Soorah Al-Baqarah (2): 61

68. Reported from him by al-Daarimee (1/45) and its chain of narration is authentic.

69. Soorah Al-A'raaf (7): 180

70. He is Abul Hasan Ahmad ibn Muhammad ibn Ja'far ibn Hamdaan, the scholar of *Fiqh*, and he was a teacher of al-Khateebul-Baghdaadee. He was born in 362H and died in 428H.

Haneefah said: "It is not right that anyone should supplicate to Allaah except by Him, and I hate that anyone should say: 'By the glory of Your Throne' or 'By the right of Your creation'."" This is also the saying of Aboo Yoosuf. Aboo Yoosuf said: "The One who gives glory to the Throne is Allaah, so I do not hate that, but I hate that anyone should say: 'By the right of so and so' or 'By the right of Your Prophets and Messengers' or 'By the right of the Sacred House, and the Sacred Area (of *Muzdalifah*).'"

Al-Qudooree said: "Asking Him by His creation is not allowed since the creation has no right over the Creator, therefore it cannot be allowed." Shaikhul-Islaam Ibn Taymiyyah reports this in *al-Qaa'idatul-Jaliyyah*.

Az-Zubaydee says in *Sharhul-Ihyaa* (2/285): "Aboo Haneefah and his two companions hated that a person should say: 'I ask You by the right of so and so' or ' By the right of Your Prophets and Messengers' or 'By the right of the Sacred House and Sacred Area (of Muzdalifah)' and the like, since no one has any right upon Allaah. Likewise Aboo Haneefah and Muhammad [ibn Hasan ash-Shaybaanee] hated that a person making supplication should say: 'O Allaah I ask You by the glory of Your Throne' and it was allowed by Aboo Yoosuf due to a report which reached him."[71]

However the report which is mentioned is baseless, and is not authentic. Ibnul-Jawzee quotes it in *al-Mawdoo'aat* and says: "This *hadeeth* is fabricated with-

---

71. I have quoted a number of these reports since many of the blind-following Hanafees and others deny the correctness of this as a saying of Aboo Haneefah, *rahimahullaah*. So if the like of this report is not established from him, then there is nothing at all that can be established from him in the books of *Fiqh*, as will not be hidden from any scholar who is aware of the way in which the sayings of the Hanafee scholars are reported in the books of their *madhhab*. Then it is extremely strange how some of them, when confronted with this saying of Aboo Haneefah they openly say that they are not bound to accept this saying of his since there are authentic *ahaadeeth* which show, as they claim, that one may call upon Allaah by means of other than Allaah, as occurs in the *hadeeth* of the people of the cave and the *hadeeth* of Buraydah. These two *ahaadeeth* have preceded and we have given the correct explanation of them. Then they=

out a doubt." Then al-Haafidh az-Zayla'ee agreed with him in *Nasbur-Raayah* (4/273) so it cannot be used as a proof. Then if the saying of a person: 'I ask You by the glory of Your Throne' is in origin *tawassul* through one of Allaah's attributes, then it is a prescribed form of *tawassul* as is shown by many other proofs, as has preceded. Therefore there is no need for this fabricated *hadeeth*. Ibnul-Atheer, *rahimahullaah*, said: "I ask You by the (source of the) glory of Your Throne. That is by those characteristics which give the Throne its glory, or the places where glory is attached to it. Its meaning in reality is: 'By the glory of Your Throne', and the companions of Aboo Haneefah hate wordings such as this in supplication." So upon the first explanation, that it refers to the characteristics which give the Throne its glory, then that would be *tawassul* by means of the attributes of Allaah, the Most High, and would be permissible. But upon the second explanation, that it refers to the places of the Throne whereby glory is attached, then that would be *tawassul* by means of something created and is not permissible. Whatever the case this *hadeeth* is not deserving of further discussion and explanation since it is not authentic, so we suffice with what has preceded.

=say this despite the fact that their methodology and well-known way is that they are drowned in *taqleed* (blind-following) up to their ears, and they turn away from any *hadeeth* which conflicts with their *madhhab*, even if the *hadeeth* has an authentic chain of narration and its meaning is clear. So how is it that they turn to our methodology here when the ways of replying to us by means of their *madhhab* is closed? Is this self contradiction from them, or is it carelessness, or is it that يَقُولُونَ بِأَلْسِنَتِهِم مَّا لَيْسَ فِى قُلُوبِهِمْ : **"They say with their tongues what is not in their hearts."**[Al-Fath (48): 11] in order to reject the truth which was stated by the imaam of their *madhhab*, just because he is in agreement with what we call them with regard to abandoning *tawassul* by means of people and seeking *tawassul* by Allaah, the Most High, and His attributes? So is it the case that they are prepared to take acting upon authentic *ahaadeeth* as their methodology in all their *Fiqh*, so that we will then require them to follow tens of, or rather hundreds of authentic *ahaadeeth* which they oppose in favour of their *madhhab*? In that case their view and our view would be the same. Or is it the case that they will only follow the *hadeeth* and differ with the *madhhab* when that goes along with their desires and interests, and that they will stick to the *madhhab* and oppose the *hadeeth*, if the *hadeeth* does not happen to satisfy their desires and interests! As for their seeking to use the *hadeeth* of Buraydah and the *hadeeth*

c h a p t e r   F O U R

Doubts Raised and their Rebuttal

The disputers raise a number of objections and doubts about this matter in order to seek to strengthen their erroneous view, and to cause the common folk to believe it to be correct, and to hide the reality of the matter from them. I will quote these doubts, in what follows, one after the other, replying to them with a reply which is according to the principles of knowledge and convincing if Allaah wills. This will confirm what has been established in the previous chapter. It will satisfy anyone who is sincere and just, and will refute all those who make false charges against us, and success and rectitude is granted by Allaah, the Most High, alone, and it is His aid that we seek.

=of the men in the cave as a proof, then that is rejected, since both of them clearly show *tawassul* by means of righteous actions, which are the testification of *Tawheed* in the first *hadeeth*; and good treatment of parents, withholding from that which is forbidden and excellent treatment of an employee in the second *hadeeth*, and this is our saying, and we do not stick blindly to the previous saying of Aboo Haneefah which apparently prevents this type of *tawassul*. Nor is it binding upon us to hold onto that if it is contrary to *hadeeth*, since with us the *hadeeth* takes precedence over his saying. So the disagreement between us and the blind-followers is due to this, which they manifest their calling this *tawassul* 'supplication to Allaah by other than Him' then this is one of their false acts of concealment of the truth, and their clear errors as will not be hidden from people of understanding.

• *the first doubt*

THE *HADEETH* DESCRIBING HOW 'UMAR USED TO REQUEST AL-'ABBAAS - *RADIYALLAAHU 'ANHUMAA,* TO PRAY FOR RAIN

They use, as an evidence for the permissibility of *tawassul* by means of a persons status, honour and right, the *hadeeth* of Anas which has preceded: "That 'Umar ibn al-Khattaab, *radiyallaahu 'anhu,* in times of drought used to ask al-'Abbaas ibn 'Abdul-Muttalib to pray for rain on their behalf. He himself would say: "O Allaah we used to ask Your Prophet to supplicate on our behalf to You and You would bless us with rain, and now we ask the uncle of our Prophet to supplicate to You on our behalf, so bless us with rain." He said: "So they would be blessed with rain."[72]

So they understand from this *hadeeth* that 'Umar, *radiyallaahu 'anhu* used to use the status of al-'Abbaas, *radiyallaahu 'anhu,* as a means of *tawassul,* and his position before Allaah. As if his *tawassul* was merely to mention the name of al-'Abbaas in his supplication and to ask Allaah to grant them rain because of that. Also that the Companions agreed to this, so this, according to their claim, proves what they hold. As for the reason why 'Umar, *radiyallaahu 'anhu* left off *tawassul* of the Messenger (ﷺ) and instead used al-'Abbaas, *radiyallaahu 'anhu* for this, then they claim that this was only in order to show the permissibility of *tawassul* by means of a person of excellence, even though there are those who are more excellent than him.

This idea of theirs is erroneous, and their explanation is rejected due to many reasons, the most important of them being:

1. A very important principle in the Islamic *Sharee'ah* is that the *Sharee'ah* texts explain one another, and none of them are to be understood about a certain matter in isolation from the rest of the texts reported about it. So upon this principle, the previous *hadeeth* about the *tawassul* of 'Umar is to

---

72. Reported by al-Bukhaaree and others.

be understood in the light of the other established narrations and *ahaadeeth* reported about *tawassul*, after they have been gathered and verified. Then both we and the disputants are agreed that there is a verbal omission[73] in the speech of 'Umar: "We used to do *tawassul* to You by means of our Prophet... and now we do *tawassul* to You by means of the uncle of our Prophet," and this omission in wording must have as its meaning either: 'We used to do *tawassul* to You by means of (the status of) our Prophet, but now we do *tawassul* to You by means of (the status of) the uncle of our Prophet', in their view, or 'We used to do *tawassul* to You by means of (the supplication of) our Prophet, but now we do *tawassul* to You by means of (the supplication of) the uncle of our Prophet', in our view. Now one of these two possible meanings must be taken in order to understand clearly what is being said.

Then in order to know which of these two possible meanings is correct we must refer back to the *Sunnah* in order to see which way of *tawassul* by means of the Prophet (ﷺ) was practised by the noble Companions. We need to look and see whether, when they suffered a drought, each of them sat in his house, or somewhere else, or came together, not in the presence of Allaah's Messenger (ﷺ) and then supplicated to their Lord, saying: 'O Allaah by Your Prophet Muhammad, and his honour before You, and his status with You, bless us with rain,' for example, or whether they used to come to the Prophet (ﷺ) in person and ask him to supplicate to Allaah, the Most High, for them, and then that he would comply with their request and supplicate to His Lord with full humility until they were blessed with rain.

As for the first of these matters then it is not to be found anywhere in the noble Prophetic *ahaadeeth*, nor in the practice of the noble Companions, *radiyallaahu 'anhum*, and there is no way that any of those in opposition to the way of the Pious Predecessors nor the followers of Sufism will be able to bring a

---

73. Translator's note: i.e. Unspoken words whose meaning is to be understood to comprehend the full meaning of the sentence.

proof to establish that their *tawassul* was to mention the name of the Prophet (ﷺ) in their supplications and to make requests to Allaah by his right and his status before Allaah. Rather what we find many examples of, and which the books of *Sunnah* are replete with is the second matter. So we find that the way in which the noble Companions of the Prophet (ﷺ) performed *tawassul* was that when they had some need, or they wished for some distress to be removed, then they would go to him (ﷺ) and ask him directly to supplicate to his Lord for them, i.e. they used the supplication of the noble Messenger (ﷺ) as a means of nearness (*tawassul*) to Allaah, the Most High, this and this alone. We are also directed to this by the Saying of Allaah, the Blessed and the Most High :

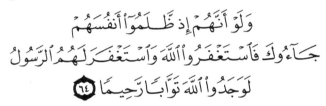

"If they (the hypocrites), when they had been unjust to themselves, had come to you (Muhammad (ﷺ)) and begged Allaah's Forgiveness, and the Messenger had begged forgiveness for them: indeed, they would have found Allaah All-Forgiving, Most Merciful."[74]

Another example of it is the *hadeeth* of Anas which has preceded which mentions the bedouin who came to the mosque on the day of *Jumu'ah* whilst the Messenger of Allaah (ﷺ) was giving the *Khutbah*. So he mentioned their difficult situation and the drought and death of their cattle, and he asked him to supplicate to Allaah, the One free of all imperfections, to save them from their predicament. So he (ﷺ) responded to this request and he is as he is described by His Lord in His Saying:

---

74. Soorah An-Nisaa (4): 64

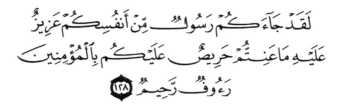

لَقَدْ جَاءَكُمْ رَسُولٌ مِّنْ أَنفُسِكُمْ عَزِيزٌ
عَلَيْهِ مَا عَنِتُّمْ حَرِيصٌ عَلَيْكُم بِالْمُؤْمِنِينَ
رَءُوفٌ رَّحِيمٌ ﴿١٢٨﴾

"Verily there has come unto you a Messenger (Muhammad (ﷺ)) from amongst yourselves. It grieves him that you should receive any injury or difficulty. He is anxious over you, for the believers (he (ﷺ)) is) full of pity, kind and merciful."[75]

So he (ﷺ) supplicated to his Lord for them, and He, the One free of all imperfections, answered the supplication of His Prophet, and showed mercy to His servants, and showered His Mercy upon them, and gave life to their barren land.

Also from this is the coming of the same bedouin or someone else on the following *Jumu'ah* to the Prophet (ﷺ) again whilst he was delivering the *Khutbah*. He then complained to him about the roads being cut off, and the collapse of houses, and drowning of cattle, and he asked him to supplicate to His Lord to withhold the rain from them. So he (ﷺ) did so and his Lord, the Most Majestic, again answered his supplication.

Another example of this is what the noble lady 'Aaishah, *radiyallaahu 'anhaa*, reports, saying: "The people complained to Allaah's Messenger(ﷺ) about the lack of rain, so he ordered for a *minbar* to be placed in the Prayer-ground, and he set a day for the people to come out. She said: So Allaah's Messenger(ﷺ) came out when the rim of the sun appeared and he sat upon the *minbar* and declared Allaah's greatness, and praised Him, and then he said: *You have com-*

---

75. Soorah At-Tawbah (9): 128

plained of drought at your abodes, and delay of rain at the start of its season, and Allaah has ordered that you supplicate to Him, and has promised that He will answer your supplication... (the hadeeth)."[76]

In the *hadeeth* it is mentioned that he (ﷺ) called upon Allaah, the One free of all imperfections, and led the people in Prayer, and that He, the Most High, granted them rain, so that the streams flowed with water, and the people hurried off to their homes, so the Messenger (ﷺ) laughed such that his molar teeth were visible and he said: *I bear witness that Allaah has full power over everything, and that I am the slave of Allaah and His Messenger.*

So these *ahaadeeth* and their like which occurred in the time of the Prophet (ﷺ) and the time of the noble Companions, *radiyallaahu 'anhum*, clarifying the matter leaving no room for argument or debate, that the *tawassul* by means of the Prophet (ﷺ) or the righteous which was practised by the Pious Predecessors was that the one seeking *tawassul* would come to the one whom he wished to use to perform *tawassul* and would ask him to supplicate to Allaah, the One free of all imperfections, in order to attain what he wished for. So he would consent to this and then Allaah, the One free of all imperfections would answer his supplication.

2.   The explanation of the meaning of *tawassul* which we have given is also what is well known from the daily lives of the people, since if one of them needs something from a manager, a president, or anyone in some position, for example, then he will look for someone who knows him who can then go to him, speak to him and mention the request of the original person, so that he will then carry it out. So this intermediary conveys his request to the one in authority who will then usually carry out what is required. This is the *'tawas-*

---

76. Reported by Aboo Daawood (translation 1/302/1169), and he said: "This is a rare *hadeeth* and its chain of narration is *saheeh*," and it is as he said, and a group of scholars have declared it authentic as I have pointed out in *Saheeh Abee Daawood* (no.1064).

sul' known to the Arabs since olden times and it is still the case. So if one of them says: *'tawassul ilaa fulaan'* (I did *'tawassul'* to so and so), then what he means is that he went to a second person and mentioned his need to him, so that he would then go and mention it to the person in authority, make the request and have it fulfilled. No one will ever understand from this that what he did was to go to the one in authority and say to him: 'By the right of (the intermediary) upon you, and his position with you, fulfil my request.'

Likewise *tawassul* to Allaah is not by means of a pious person's station or his right, but it is by means of his supplication and his humbly beseeching Allaah, the One free of all imperfections and the Most High, and earnestly requesting His aid.

This is also the meaning of the saying of 'Umar, *radiyallaahu 'anhu*: "O Allaah we used to do *tawassul* to You by means of our Messenger and You would bless us with rain...," meaning: When there was a drought, for example, we used to go to the Prophet (ﷺ) to supplicate to Allaah, the Majestic, for us.

3.   This is further emphasised and clarified by the completion of the saying of 'Umar, *radiyallaahu 'anhu*: "... and now we use the uncle of our Prophet to do *tawassul* to You, so bless us with rain." Meaning that after the death of our Prophet (ﷺ) we come with al-'Abbaas, the uncle of the Prophet (ﷺ) and we ask him to supplicate for us to our Lord, the One free of all imperfections, that he should bless us with rain.

As for the question as to why 'Umar, *radiyallaahu 'anhu* changed from *tawassul* by means of the Prophet (ﷺ) to *tawassul* by means of al-'Abbaas, *radiyallaahu 'anhu*, despite the fact that al-'Abbaas even though he has high status and rank, yet that is no way carries precedence over the status and rank of the Prophet (ﷺ).

The answer to this is, in our view, that *tawassul* by means of the Prophet (ﷺ) is not possible after his death. since how could they go to him (ﷺ), explain their condition, and ask him to supplicate for them, and for them to say '*Aameen*'[77] to it, when he has passed on to the company of the highest angels, and entered a state of existence so different from this worldly life and state such that it is known to nobody except Allaah, the One free of all imperfections and the Most High? So how can they now attain a share of his supplication and intercession for them when there is between them and him, as Allaah says:

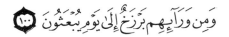

"...and behind them is *barzakh* (a barrier) until the Day when they will be resurrected."[78]

Therefore 'Umar, *radiyallaahu 'anhu*, who was of pure Arabian descent and who was a Companion of the Prophet (ﷺ) and accompanied him most of the time, and knew him very well, and fully understood his religion, and on a number of occasions *Aayaat* of the Quraan were sent down in confirmation of his view; he employed a means of *tawassul* which was something possible, choosing al-'Abbaas, *radiyallaahu 'anhu*, due to his being a close relative of the Prophet (ﷺ) and also because of his righteousness, practice of the religion and his piety, and he asked him to supplicate for them for rain. Furthermore it would not be fitting for 'Umar, nor anyone other than 'Umar to abandon *tawassul* by means of the Prophet (ﷺ) and to turn instead to *tawassul* by means of al-'Abbaas if it were still possible to carry out *tawassul* by means of the Prophet (ﷺ). Nor can it be imagined that all of the Companions, *radiyallaahu 'anhum*, would agree to that if 'Umar had done it, since leaving *tawassul* by means of the Prophet (ﷺ) in favour of *tawassul* by means of others would be just like leaving following the Prophet (ﷺ) in Prayer in favour of fol-

---

77. Translator's note: Meaning, "O Allaah, respond to it."
78. Soorah Al-Muminoon (23): 100

lowing someone else; it is just the same. Rather the Companions, *radiyallaahu 'anhum*, knew fully the honour, status and excellence of their Prophet (ﷺ) and that no one else could in any way approach that status. We find this clearly illustrated in the *hadeeth* of Sahl ibn Sa'd as-Saa'idee, *radiyallaahu 'anhu*: "That Allaah's Messenger (ﷺ) went to Banoo 'Amr ibn 'Awf in order to bring reconciliation between them. So the time of Prayer came and the *muadhdhin* came to Aboo Bakr and said: "Will you lead the Prayer, so that I may pronounce the *Iqaamah*?" So Aboo Bakr led the people in Prayer. Then Allaah's Messenger (ﷺ) came whilst the people were praying, so he came through the rows until he stood in the (first) row and the people clapped their hands. Aboo Bakr did not, however, glance aside. But when the people continued to clap their hands he glanced and saw Allaah's Messenger (ﷺ). Allaah's Messenger (ﷺ) indicated for him to remain at his place, but Aboo Bakr raised his hands and praised Allaah, the Mighty and Majestic, for the order of Allaah's Messenger (ﷺ). Then Aboo Bakr retreated into the first row and the Prophet (ﷺ) went forward and lead the Prayer. When he finished he said: *O Aboo Bakr what prevented you from remaining at your place when I ordered you?* Aboo Bakr said: "It is not fitting for the son of Ibn Abee Quhaafah to lead the Prayer in the presence of Allaah's Messenger (ﷺ).""[79]

So you see that the Companions, *radiyallaahu 'anhum*, did not deem it proper that they should continue to be led in Prayer by Aboo Bakr, *radiyallaahu 'anhu* when the Messenger (ﷺ) was present, just as Aboo Bakr, *radiyallaahu 'anhu* could not bring himself to remain at his place when the Prophet (ﷺ) told him to. Why? All of this was due to the esteem which they had for their Prophet (ﷺ) and their manners in his presence and their recognition of his rights and his honour. So if the Companions were not pleased except that they should be led in the Prayer by the Prophet (ﷺ) when that was possible, even though they had begun the Prayer when he (ﷺ) was absent, then how

---

79. Reported by al-Bukhaaree (translation 1/368/no.652) and Muslim (translation 1/233/no.845).

should they abandon *tawassul* by means of him after his death if it were something possible, and instead prefer *tawassul* by means of someone else? Furthermore just as Aboo Bakr could not accept that he should lead the people in Prayer, then it is self-evident that al-'Abbaas would also not accept the peoples performing *tawassul* by means of him, and the abandoning *tawassul* by means of the Prophet (ﷺ), if that were at all possible.

NOTE: From another angle this also shows the foolish thinking of those who claim that he (ﷺ) is living in his grave with a life just the same as our life. If this were the case then there would be no acceptable reason at all for them to abandon being led in Prayer by him, and instead being led in Prayer by others, who do not in any way reach his position and excellence. Then this is not to be objected to by the fact that it is reported that the Prophet(ﷺ) said: *I am alive and fresh in my grave; whoever gives me the greetings of 'salaam' then I will give the greeting of 'salaam' to him*. Nor by the fact that they say that this means that he is alive with a life which is just the same as our life, so that if we use him as a means of *tawassul* he will then hear and respond to us, so that we attain our goal and what we desire. They further claim that there is no difference in all of this between his (ﷺ) condition during his lifetime and his condition after his death. Then to all this I say: No one can use this as an objection since it is rejected from two angles: The first, according to the science of *hadeeth*. This is because this '*hadeeth*' has no basis at all with this wording. Likewise the wording (*tariyy*) 'fresh' in not found in a number of authentic *ahaadeeth*, from them his (ﷺ) saying: *From the most excellent of your days is the day of Jumu'ah. On it Aadam was created, and on it his soul was taken, and on it will be the blowing of the Horn, and on it the Tremendous Cry will occur, so send more blessings (salaat) upon me on it, since your blessings will be presented to me*. They said: 'O Messenger of Allaah, how will our blessings be presented to you when your body has decayed?' He said: *Allaah has forbidden the earth from consuming the bodies of the Prophets*.[80]

---

80 Reported by Aboo Daawood (translation 1/269/no.1042), an-Nasaa'ee and others from the *hadeeth* of Aws ibn Aws and its chain of narration is *saheeh*.

From them also are his (ﷺ) sayings: *The Prophets are alive and pray in their graves.*[81]

On the night when I was taken up through the Heavens I passed by Moosaa and he was standing in Prayer in his grave.[82]

Indeed Allaah has Angels who travel about in order to convey the greetings of salaam of my Ummah to me.[83]

The second reply is from the *Fiqh* angle: In essence it is that his (ﷺ) life after his death is different to his life before his death. That if because the after-life between death and the resurrection (*al-hayaatul-barzakhiyyah*) is part of the world of the Hidden and the Unseen. None knows how it is except for Allaah, the One free of all imperfections and the Most High. However what is known and established is that it is different from the worldly life, and not subject to its laws and criteria. So in the worldly life the person eats and drinks, breathes and marries, moves and uses the toilet, falls ill and speaks. But no one can establish that these things are also common to people after death, not even the prophets, *'alaihimus-salaam*, and at the head of them is our Prophet Muhammad (ﷺ). This is emphasised by the fact that the Companions differed about many matters after his (ﷺ) death, and none of them ever thought of going to him (ﷺ) in his grave and asking his advice and asking about what was correct. Why not? The matter is very clear, all of them knew that he (ﷺ) had left behind this worldly life and its conditions and affairs. So after his death Allaah's Messenger (ﷺ) is indeed alive, living the most perfect life that any person lives between death and the Resurrection. However it is a life which

81 Reported by Aboo Ya'laa and al-Bazzaar and others from Anas ibn Maalik and its chain of narration is *saheeh* and it can be found in my book *Silsilatul-Ahaadeethis-Saheehah* (no.62).

82 Reported by Ahmad, Muslim (translation 4/1266/no.5858), also from Anas ibn Maalik.

83 Reported by an-Nasaa'ee, ad-Daarimee, Ibn Hibbaan and al-Haakim (2/21) from Ibn Mas'ood, and (al-Haakim) declared it *saheeh* and adh-Dhahabee and Ibn Hibbaan agreed, and it is as they said. It can be found in *al-Mishkaat* (no.924) and *Fadlus-Salaat 'alan-Nabee* (no.21).

does not resemble the life of this life and perhaps that can be seen from his
(ﷺ) saying: *No one gives me greetings of salaam except that Allaah will
restore my soul to me so that I may reply to him with the greeting of salaam.*[84]

In any case its reality is known only to Allaah, the One free of all imperfections
and the Most High. Therefore it is not permissible to make analogy between
the After-life before the Resurrection or the Hereafter and this worldly life, just
as it is not permissible to apply the rulings of one to the other. Rather each of
them has its own particular characteristics and its own rules. There is no similarity except in name and as for the reality of that life, then it is known only to
Allaah, the Blessed and Most High.

After making this point we return to the reply to the disputants concerning
'Umar's *tawassul* by means of al-'Abbaas, and we say: Their explanation of the
reason why 'Umar turned away from *tawassul* by means of the Prophet (ﷺ)
to *tawassul* by means of al-'Abbaas, *radiyallaahu 'anhu*, to be that it was in
order to show the permissibility of *tawassul* by means of someone excellent
even though there is someone more excellent present. Then we say this is an
amazing and laughable explanation. This is because how is it possible that such
a thing could enter the mind of 'Umar, *radiyallaahu 'anhu*, or anyone of the
noble Companions, *radiyallaahu 'anhum*? How could this hair-splitting idea
of the late comers have entered his mind, when he saw the people in such a
distressed and difficult situation, a situation of suffering and grief, when they
were on the point of death due to hunger and thirst due to the lack of water,
death of cattle, and absence of crops and greenery upon the earth, to the point
that the year in question was called 'the year of drought/destruction'. How
could this philosophical point cross his mind in these difficult circumstances,
so that he would leave the major means of *tawassul* in his supplication, i.e.
tawassul by means of the greatest Messenger (ﷺ), even if it were permissi-

---

84. Reported by Aboo Daawood (translation 2/542/no.2036) from Aboo Hurairah with a good
(*hasan*) chain of narration, and it is to be found in my book *as-Saheehah* (no.2266)...

ble, and instead seek to employ the lesser means of *tawassul* which cannot be compared to the first, making *tawassul* by means of al-'Abbaas? Why? For nothing except to explain to the people that it was permissible for them to make *tawassul* by means of someone excellent even in the presence of someone who was more excellent?!

As is well-known and witnessed if a person is in distress he tries to use the strongest means he can to repel it and leaves all other means for times of ease. This was even a fact understood by the idol-worshippers in the days of ignorance. In times of ease they used to call upon their idols, yet in times of difficulty they would abandon them and call upon Allaah, the Most High, alone. As He, the Blessed and the Most High, says:

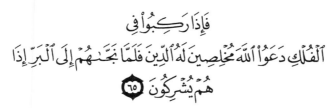

"And when they embark on a ship they invoke Allaah, making their faith pure for Him only, but when He brings them safely to land, behold, they give a share of their worship to others."[85]

So we know from this that the human by his inborn nature will in times of distress and need seek the help of the greatest possible strength and the strongest means. Then in times of safety and ease he may sometimes turn to lesser means and at those times it might cross ones mind to make clear the *Fiqh* ruling which they have proposed, i.e. that it is permissible to seek to perform *tawassul* by means of someone excellent despite the presence of one who is more excellent. A further matter that we mention in reply to the doubts

85. Al-'Ankaboot (29): 65

of those people is that even if we were to accept that it crossed the mind of 'Umar, *radiyallaahu 'anhu*, to explain this *Fiqh* ruling which they claim, then do you think that it had also crossed the mind of Mu'aawiyah and ad-Dahhaak ibn Qays when they made *tawassul* by means of the noble *Tabi'ee* Yazeed ibn al-Aswad al-Jurashee? There is no doubt that this is merely an exercise in seeking to use cunning to support their far-fetched ideas, and not something which they are to be envied for.

4.   We also find in the *hadeeth* mentioning 'Umar's request to al-'Abbaas, *radiyallaahu 'anhumaa*, a point which is very important to mention, and it is his saying: "In times of drought 'Umar used to ask al-'Abbaas ibn 'Abdul-Muttalib to pray for rain for them." So this indicates that 'Umar's requesting al-'Abbaas, *radiyallaahu 'anhumaa*, to pray for rain was repeated a number of times, and this contains a very clear proof against those who wrongly interpret the action of 'Umar, in abandoning *tawassul* by means of the Prophet (ﷺ) in favour of *tawassul* by means of his uncle, saying that he did it to show the permissibility of doing *tawassul* by means of one possessing excellence even if one more excellent is available. Then we say that even if it were the case then he would have done that once and not continually, every time they prayed for rain. This is very clear indeed and will not be hidden, if Allaah the Most High wills, from people of knowledge and fairness.

5.   Some of the authentic narrations explain the aforementioned words of 'Umar and his attention. These narrations quote the supplication of al-'Abbaas, *radiyallaahu 'anhu*, which he made in response to the request of 'Umar, *radiyallaahu 'anhu*. From them is what al-Haafidh al-'Asqalaanee, *rahimahullaah*, reports in *al-Fath* (3/150), saying: "Az-Zubayr ibn al-Bakkaar mentions in *al-Ansaab* the description of the supplication of al-'Abbaas at this occasion and at that time, so he reports with his chain of narration that al-'Abbaas when requested by 'Umar to pray for rain, said: "O Allaah no misfortune descends except due to sins, and is not removed except through repentance, and the people turn to You by means of me due to my position with

regard to Your Prophet. Here are our hands turned to You with our sins, and our forelocks turned to You in repentance. So bless us with a downpour of rain." He said: So the heavens released rain like the mountains, the earth became fertile and the people lived." This *hadeeth* shows:

(i) That the *tawassul* was by means of supplication of al-'Abbaas, *radiyal-laahu 'anhu*, not by his person, as was explained by az-Zubayr ibn Bakkaar and others. So this contains a clear reply to those who claim that the *tawassul* of 'Umar was by means of the person of al-'Abbaas and not his supplication, since if that were true then there would be no need for al-'Abbaas to stand up and supplicate anew after the supplication of 'Umar.

(ii) That 'Umar clearly stated that they used to do *tawassul* by means of the Prophet (ﷺ) in his lifetime, and that in this instance he was now doing *tawassul* by means of his uncle al-'Abbaas. So this leaves no room for doubt about the fact that these were both instances of the same type of *tawassul*, both the *tawassul* by means of the Messenger (ﷺ) and the *tawassul* by means of al-'Abbaas. So when it is clear to the reader, as will follow, that their *tawassul* by means of the Prophet (ﷺ) was *tawassul* by means of his supplication, then this means that their *tawassul* by means of al-'Abbaas was also by means of his supplication, since both these examples of *tawassul* were of the same type. As for the proof that their *tawassul* by means of the Prophet (ﷺ) was *tawassul* by means of his supplication for them, then the proof of this is clearly shown in the narration of al-Ismaa'eelee in his *Mustakhraj 'alas-Saheeh* of this *hadeeth* with the wording: "In times of drought in the time of the Prophet (ﷺ) they used to seek rain through him, so he would pray for rain for them, then in the time of 'Umar..." and he mentioned the rest of the *hadeeth*. I have quoted this from *al-Fath* (2/399). So his saying: "So he would pray for rain for them" clearly shows that he (ﷺ) asked Allaah, the Most High, to send rain to them. As occurs in *an-Nihaayah* of Ibnul-Atheer: "*al-Istisqaa* means requesting rain, i.e. that rain should be sent down upon the land and the worshippers... and *istasqaita fulaanan* means: that you requested so and so to send rain to you."

When this is clear, then his saying in this narration: "They sought rain through him" means by means of his supplication and it is not possible to understand anything except this from the combined narrations of the *hadeeth*. Then it is further supported by:

(iii) If it were the case that the *tawassul* of 'Umar was by the person of al-'Abbaas, or his status before Allaah, the Most High, then he would not have abandoned similar *tawassul* by means of the Prophet (ﷺ), since this would be possible if it were prescribed in the *Sharee'ah*. So the fact that 'Umar left *tawassul* by means of the Messenger (ﷺ) in favour of *tawassul* by means of the supplication of al-'Abbaas, *radiyallaahu 'anhu*, is the greatest proof that 'Umar and the Companions who were with him had not used to hold that there was any such thing as *tawassul* by means of his (ﷺ) person. Then the practice of the Pious Predecessors continued in like manner after them, as you have seen from the *tawassul* of Mu'aawiyah ibn al-Aswad al-Jurashee. These two occurrences very clearly demonstrate that what he did was to supplicate (*du'aa*).

So would it be permissible that all of them should gather together in abandoning *tawassul* by means of his (ﷺ) person if it were something allowable? Especially since the antagonists claim that it is something better than *tawassul* by means of the supplication of al-'Abbaas or anyone else?! By Allaah that would not be permissible, nor acceptable to the intellect. Rather this *ijmaa'* (consensus) of theirs is one of the greatest proofs that the aforesaid *tawassul* [i.e. by means of his (ﷺ) person] was something that was not prescribed in their view, since they were more excellent than that they should replace that which is good with that which is not as good!

AN OBJECTION AND ITS REBUTTAL

As regards the reply of the author of *Misbaahuz-Zujaajah fee Fawaa'id Qadaa'il-Haajah* to the question of why 'Umar would have abandoned *tawassul* by means of the person of the Prophet (ﷺ), then he said: "'Umar did not hear of the *hadeeth* of the *tawassul* of the blind man (see p.68 for the text of the *hadeeth*), and if it had reached him then he would have done *tawassul* by means of him (ﷺ)." Then this is futile from a number of angles:

F i r s t : That the *hadeeth* of the blind man shows the same thing as this *hadeeth* about the *tawassul* of 'Umar, i.e. that it was *tawassul* by means of his supplication, not his person, as has preceded.

S e c o n d : The *tawassul* of 'Umar was nothing done in secret, rather it was done openly in front of the people, amongst them being some of the major Companions from the *Muhaajiroon*, the *Ansaar* and others. So even if it was possible that the *hadeeth* was unknown to 'Umar, then can it be possible that it was also unknown to all the Companions who were present along with 'Umar?!

T h i r d : That 'Umar, as has preceded, used to repeat this *tawassul* whenever there was a situation of danger for the people of al-Madeenah, or whenever they needed to pray for rain, as is shown by the wording 'He used to ...' in the previous *hadeeth* of Anas: "That when there was a drought 'Umar used to ask al-'Abbaas to pray for rain for them." The same is reported by Ibn 'Abbaas from 'Umar as Ibn 'Abdul-Barr mentions in *al-Istee'aab* (3/98), so even if that could be unknown to him the first time, then is it possible that he could remain ignorant of that every time he asked al-'Abbaas to pray for rain for them, and in the presence of the *Muhaajiroon* and the *Ansaar*, and that they remained silent and did not put forward the knowledge they had of the *hadeeth* of the blind-man?! By Allaah, such a reply would be an accusation of ignorance of the *hadeeth* of the blind-man against all of the Companions, or at least of their lack of knowledge of the fact that it is a proof for *tawassul* by his person. The first is obviously totally false, and the second is true, since if they had known that the *hadeeth* of the blind-man proved the form of *tawassul* which they claim, then they would not in that case have abandoned *tawassul* by means of his (ﷺ) person in favour of *tawassul* by means of the supplication of al-'Abbaas, as has preceded.

F o u r t h : 'Umar was not alone in preferring *tawassul* by means of his (ﷺ) supplication to *tawassul* by means of his person, rather the same was done by Mu'aawiyah ibn Abee Sufyaan who also performed *tawassul* by means of the supplication of Yazeed ibn al-Aswad and not by means of the Prophet (ﷺ), and a number of the Companions and greater *tabi'een* were present with him. So is it to be said also that Mu'aawiyah and those who were present with him did not know of the *hadeeth* of the blind-man? Then are we to also say the same about the *tawassul* of ad-Dahhaak ibn Qays with Yazeed also?

The author of *al-Misbaah* gives another reply, and he is followed in it by one of the blind-following antagonists who are deprived of correctness, saying: "What 'Umar intended by his *tawassul* by means of al-'Abbaas was to follow the examples of the Prophet (ﷺ) in honouring and showing respect to al-'Abbaas. The like of this is clearly stated by 'Umar. Az-Zubayr ibn Bakkaar reports in *al-Ansaab*, by way of Daawood ibn 'Ataa, from Zayd ibn Aslam, from Ibn 'Umar who said: "In the year of famine/destruction 'Umar ibn al-Khattaab sought rain by means of al-'Abbaas, so 'Umar gave a *khutbah* and said: "Indeed Allaah's Messenger (ﷺ) used to regard al-'Abbaas just as a son regards his father, so O people follow the example of Allaah's Messenger (ﷺ) and take him as a means of attaining nearness to Allaah..." It is also reported by al-Balaadhuree by way of Hishaam ibn Sa'd from Zayd ibn Aslam from his father."

Then the reply to this is also from a number of angles:

F i r s t : We do not accept the authenticity of this narration since it is report-ed by way of Daawood ibn 'Ataa who is al-Madanee, and he is weak (*da'eef*) as occurs in *at-Taqreeb*, and it is reported from him by az-Zubayr ibn Bakkaar as al-Haakim (3/334) reports it, and is silent about it. Adh-Dhahabee however crit-icises this by his saying "Daawood is abandoned (*matrook*)." I say: The narra-tor from him is Saa'idah ibn 'Ubaydullaah al-Muzaanee and I do not find any biography for him. Then there is also contradiction (*idtiraab*) between its chain of narration, since it has been reported, as you have seen, by Hishaam ibn Sa'd, from Zayd ibn Aslam, that he said: "from his father" instead of "from Ibn 'Umar." However Hishaam is more reliable than Daawood, but we do not find his wording in order to see if it has any contradiction with the wording of Daawood or not. Then you should not be fooled by their saying in *al-Misbaah* after this chain of narration: "with it," which gives the impression that they both have the same wording, since his basis for what he quotes from al-Balaadhuree is only *Fathul-Baaree* whose author did not say "with it" [see *Fathul-Baaree* (2/399)].

S e c o n d : Even if this narration were authentic, then all it would show is the reason for which 'Umar performed *tawassul* by means of al-'Abbaas, instead of by means of the other Companions who were present at the time. But as for its showing the permissibility of turning away from *tawassul* by his (ﷺ) person, if it were permissible with them, to *tawassul* by means of al-'Abbaas, (i.e. by means of his person), then it shows no such thing at all, since we know by necessity and as is self-evident that if a group of people were struck with severe drought and they wanted to put one of them forward for them to make *tawassul*, then it would not be possible for them to turn away from one whose supplication was more likely to be answered, and who was closer to the mercy of his Lord, the One free of all imperfections and the Most High. Also if a person were struck with some serious calamity and he had before him a Prophet and someone else who was not a Prophet, and he wanted to request one of them to supplicate for him, he would not request except the Prophet. Then if he did ask the one who was not a Prophet instead, and abandoned the Prophet he would be counted as being an ignorant and sinful person. So how can it be imagined about 'Umar and the Companions with him that they would turn away from *tawassul* by means of the Prophet (ﷺ) in favour of *tawassul* by means of someone else, if *tawassul* by means of his (ﷺ) person were lawful? So how could that be the case when to the antagonists it is better than *tawassul* by means of the supplication of al-'Abbaas or any other pious person?! Especially when that was done a number of times as has preceded, and they did not seek to use him as a means of *tawassul* even once, and that was something which was repeated afterwards also. Despite this none of them did anything different to what 'Umar did. Indeed what is reported from Mu'aawiyah and those who were with him fully agrees with his practice since they sought to use as a means of *tawassul,* the supplication of the noble *tabi'ee* Yazeed ibn al-Aswad. Therefore can it be correct to say that seeking *tawassul* by means of his person was what was done in order to follow the example of the Prophet (ﷺ)?! Rather the truth is that the continuing practice of the Companions in leaving *tawassul* by means of his (ﷺ) person when they suffered hardship, after they had not used to seek *tawassul* by means of anyone else during his (ﷺ) lifetime, is indeed one of the clearest and strongest proofs that *tawassul* by means of his (ﷺ) person is not prescribed. Otherwise it would indeed have been reported from them by many chains of narrations about a number of events. Do you not see how the antagonists turn to *tawassul* by means of his (ﷺ) person at the slightest incentive since they think it to be something prescribed?!

If this were indeed the case then its like would be reported from the Companions, especially since they had greater respect and love for him (ﷺ) than the later people. Then how could this not be reported from them at all, not even a single example. Rather what is reported from them is avoidance of it in favour of *tawassul* by means of the supplication of the pious people!

• *t h e   s e c o n d   d o u b t*
THE *HADEETH* OF THE BLIND MAN

After completing our verification of what is correct with regard to the *hadeeth* about the *tawassul* of 'Umar by means of al-'Abbaas, *radiyallaahu 'anhumaa,* and showing that there is no proof in it for the disputants, rather that it is a proof against them, we will now examine what is correct about the *hadeeth* of the blind man. We will consider its meaning and see whether it is a proof for them or a further proof against them.

It is reported by Ahmad and others with an authentic chain of narration from 'Uthmaan ibn Haneef: "That a blind man came to the Prophet (ﷺ) and said, "Supplicate to Allaah that He should cure me." So he said, *If you wish I will supplicate for you and if you wish I will delay that, for that is better (and in a narration: and if you wish have patience and that is better for you).* So he said, "Supplicate to Him." So he ordered him to make *wudoo,* and to make *wudoo* well, and to pray two *rak'ahs,* and to supplicate with this *du'aa, O Allaah I ask You and turn to You by means of Your Prophet Muhammad,*[86] *the Prophet of mercy, O Muhammad I have turned by means of you (i.e. your du'aa) to my Lord in this need of mine, so that it may be fulfilled for me, O Allaah accept him as a supplicant on my behalf, and accept my supplication for him (to be accepted for me).*" He said, "So the man did it and he was cured."[87]

---

86. i.e. by means of his *du'aa,* as will be seen.

87. It is reported in *al-Musnad* (4/138) and by at-Tirmidhee (4/281-282...), Ibn Maajah (1/418), at-Tabaraanee in *al-Kabeer* (3/2/2) and al-Haakim (1/313)... all of them through 'Uthmaan ibn 'Umar (Ahmad's Shaikh in it) from Shu'bah from Aboo Ja'far al-Madanee, who said, "I heard 'Ammaarah ibn Khuzaimah narrate from 'Uthmaan with it. At-Tirmidhee said, *hasan saheeh ghareeb,* and in Ibn Maajah there occurs after it: "Aboo Ishaaq said, A *saheeh hadeeth.* Then Ahmad reports it, "Shu'bah narrated it to us, and it contains the other narration, and he is followed in that by Muhammad ibn Ja'far: Shu'bah narrated to us. Al-Haakim reported it (1/519) and said, *saheeh* of *isnaad,* and adh-Dhahabee agreed. Some of them declare that it contains weakness, such as the author of *Siyaahatul-insaan* and the author of *Tatheerul-Janaan* (p.37) and others, in that its *isnaad* contains Aboo Ja'far, At-Tirmidhee says, "We do not know it except through this chain, from the *hadeeth* of Aboo Ja'far, and he is not al-Khatamee." So they say, "Therefore he is ar-Raazee who is truthful but has poor memory." I say: That is rejected by the fact that what is correct is that he is in fact al-Khatamee, and this is what Ahmad calls him in the narration (4/138) and in the other he calls him Aboo Ja'far al-Madanee, and likewise does al-Haakim, and it is al-Khatamee who is 'al-Madanee' not ar-Raazee. This is how it is reported in at-Tabaraanee's *Mu'jamus-Sagheer* and in the Boolaq edition of at-Tirmidhee also. And that is confirmed definitely by the fact that it is al-Khatamee who narrates from 'Ammaarah ibn Khuzaimah, and from whom Shu'bah, reports, as is the case in this *isnaad,* and he is *Sadooq* (generally acceptable). Therefore this *isnaad* is good, having no obscurity.

The opponents hold that this *hadeeth* shows that it is permissible to make *tawassul* in *du'aa* by the status of the Prophet (ﷺ) or other pious people, since the Prophet (ﷺ) taught the blind man to use him as a means of nearness in his *du'aa*, and the blind man did that and his sight was restored.

As for us, than we hold that the *hadeeth* has no proof for them concerning this form of *tawassul* about which there is disagreement, which is seeking nearness by means of his person. Rather it is a further proof for the third type of lawful and prescribed *tawassul* which we have spoken of previously, since the *tawassul* of the blind man was through means of his (ﷺ) *du'aa*, and the proofs for what we say are many in the *hadeeth* itself, most importantly:

1.   The reason the blind man came to the Prophet (ﷺ) was for him to make supplication (*du'aa*) for him, as he said, "Supplicate Allaah that He should cure me." So he sought to use his (ﷺ) *du'aa* as a means of nearness to Allaah, the Most High, since he knew that his (ﷺ) supplication was more likely to be accepted by Allaah than the *du'aa* of others, and if the intention of the blind man was to seek nearness to Allaah by means of the Prophet's (ﷺ) person or status or his right, then he would have had no need to go to the Prophet (ﷺ), or to ask him to make *du'aa* for him, rather he would have sat in his house, and supplicated to his Lord saying, for example, "O Allaah I ask You by the status of Your Prophet and his station with You, that You cure me and enable me to see."

But that is not what he did. Why? Since he was an Arab and knew very well the meaning of *tawassul* in the Arabic language, and knew that it was not a word said by a person with a need, mentioning the name of a person as an intermediary, rather it had to include coming to one whom he believed to be pious and have knowledge of the Book and the *Sunnah* and ask him to make *du'aa* for him.

2.   The Prophet (ﷺ) promised that he would make *du'aa* for him, after advising him of what would be better for him, and this was his (ﷺ) saying, *If you wish I will supplicate for you, and if you wish have patience, that is better for you.* And this second matter is what he (ﷺ) indicated in the *hadeeth* which he narrated from his Lord, the Blessed and Most High, that He said, *"When I afflict My servant in his two beloved ones, that is his eyes, and he has patience, then I give him Paradise in place of them."* [Reported by al-Bukhaaree (transl. 7/377/no.557) from Anas, quoted in *as-Saheehah* (2010)]

3.   The blind man's insistence that he (ﷺ) should supplicate for him, as he said, "Supplicate to Him." Which means that the Messenger (ﷺ) definitely did make *du'aa* for him, since he (ﷺ) was the best at fulfilling a promise and he had already promised to make *du'aa* for him if he wished as has preceded, and he wanted *du'aa* from him, and so the point is established. Also the Prophet (ﷺ), out of his mercy and desire that Allaah, the Most High, should answer his *du'aa* for him, guided the blind man to using the second type of lawful and prescribed *tawassul* also, which is *tawassul* by means of righteous actions, in order to combine the different types of good.

So he (ﷺ) ordered him to make *wudoo* and to pray two *rak'ahs*, and then to make *du'aa* for himself, and these acts of obedience to Allaah, the One free of all blemish or defect, and the Most High, which he offered along with the *du'aa* of the Prophet (ﷺ) on his behalf, and this falls under Allaah, the Most High's Saying:

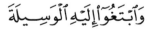

"Seek the means of approach (waseelah) to Him."[88]

as has preceded.

---

88. Soorah Al-Maaidah (5): 35

The Messenger (ﷺ) did not suffice with making *du'aa* for the blind man, as he had promised, he also gave him an action to perform which involved obedience to Allaah, the One free of all blemish and defect, the Most High, and drawing near to Him, so that the affair would be complete from all angles, and nearer to acceptance and being pleasing to Allaah, the One free of all blemish and imperfections, and the Most High, therefore the whole event revolved around *du'aa*, as is clear and contains nothing of what they mention.

Shaikh al-Ghumaaree is ignorant of this or pretends to be, since he says in *al-Misbaah* (24), "... *If you wish I will make du'aa*, means, 'If you wish I will teach you a *du'aa* which you can make and will repeat it to you,' this explanation is binding so that the start of the *hadeeth* agrees with its end."

I say: This explanation is futile due to many reasons, from them that the blind man asked him (ﷺ) to make *du'aa* for him, not to teach him a *du'aa*, and since his (ﷺ) saying to him, *And if you wish I will make du'aa*, was an answer for his request, it was then definitely a request for *du'aa*, and this has to be, and this is the meaning which agrees with the end of the *hadeeth*, which is why we find that al-Ghumaaree does not try to explain his saying at the end, *O Allaah accept him as a supplicant for me, and accept my supplication for him (to be accepted for me)*, since this clearly shows that his *tawassul* was through the *du'aa* of the Prophet (ﷺ) as we have shown in what has preceded.

Then he says, "Even if we admit that the Prophet (ﷺ) made *du'aa* for the blind man, then that does not prevent those *hadeeth* from being generalised to include others."

I say: This is clear error, since no one prevents the *hadeeth* from applying to other then the blind man, from those whom the Prophet (ﷺ) made *du'aa* for. However since *du'aa* from him (ﷺ) after he left to join the highest company is something that those seeking *tawassul* for all various needs and desires do not know about, and also they themselves do not seek *tawassul* by his (ﷺ) *du'aa* after his death, therefore the ruling is different, and this admission of al-Ghumaaree is a proof against him.

4.   In the *du'aa* which Allaah's Messenger (ﷺ) taught him to say there occurs, *O Allaah accept him as a supplicant for me*, and it is impossible to take this to mean *tawassul* by his (ﷺ) person, or his status, or his right, since the meaning is "O Allaah accept his (ﷺ) supplication for You to restore my sight."

Shafaa'ah in the language means: *du'aa*, and this is what is meant by the *shafaa'ah* which is established for him (ﷺ) and for the other Prophets and the Pious on the Day of Resurrection. This shows that *shafaa'ah* is more particular than *du'aa* since it will only occur if there are two people seeking a matter, so that one of them is a supplicant for the other, as opposed to a single person seeking something who does not bring anyone else as a supplicant for him, as occurs in *Lisaanul-'Arab*:

"*SHAFAA'AH* (INTERCEDING): is the intercessor's speaking to a king about a need which he is requesting for someone else, and the intercessor is the one seeking something for someone else, through whom he intercedes to attain what is desired..."

So it is established by this means also, that the *tawassul* of the blind man was through his (ﷺ) *du'aa*, not his person.

5.   From what the Prophet (ﷺ) taught the blind man to say was, *and accept my supplication for him (to be accepted)*[89], i.e. accept my *shafaa'ah*

---

89. This sentence is an authentic part of the *hadeeth*. It is reported by Ahmad and al-Haakim, who authenticated it, and adh-Dhahabee agrees, and it alone is a decisive proof that taking the *hadeeth* to refer to *tawassul* by his person is futile, that being the position of some recent writers. It seems that they realise this point and therefore do not mention this sentence at all,=

for him i.e. accept my *du'aa* that You accept his (ﷺ) *shafaa'ah*, i.e. his *du'aa* that You restore my sight, and it is not possible to understand anything but this from the sentence. This is why you find the opponents feigning ignorance of it and not making any mention of it since it demolishes their building from the foundations and tears down its walls, and when they hear it you will see them looking like one in a swoon.

This is because they think that they understand the *shafaa'ah* of the Messenger (ﷺ) for the blind man, but what can the blind man's *shafaa'ah* for the Messenger (ﷺ) mean? They have no answer for that at all. The fact that they perceive that this sentence nullifies their misinterpretation is shown by the fact that you will not find a single one of them using it in practice, i.e. supplicating, "O Allaah accept Your Prophet's *shafaa'ah* for me and my *shafaa'ah* for him."

6. The scholars mention this *hadeeth* amongst the miracles of the Prophet (ﷺ) and amongst his *du'aa* which were answered, and that Allaah caused miracles and the sick to be cured through the blessings of his (ﷺ) *du'aa*, because through his (ﷺ) *du'aa* for this blind man Allaah restored his sight to him.

Therefore the authors quote it amongst the signs of his Prophethood, such as al-Baihaqee and others. So this shows that the reason behind why the blind man came to be cured was the supplication of the Prophet (ﷺ) and this is further shown by all those blind people who call upon Allaah, the Most High, alone, turning to Him sincerely to be cured through it. If the other peoples understanding were true,[90]

=which shows how far they can be trusted in reporting quotations. Close to this is their quoting the previous sentence, O *Allaah accept his shafaa'ah for me*, as a proof for *tawassul* by his person, but as for explaining how it shows that then they do not explain that to the readers, since one not possessing something cannot give it to others.

90. i.e. If it were the case that the blind man was cured because he used the *du'aa* and made *tawassul* by the person of the Prophet(ﷺ), as these people claim!

then at least one of them would have been cured, and this is something that does not happen, and perhaps never happens.

Also if the reason for the blind man's cure was that he did *tawassul* through the status of the Prophet(ﷺ) and position and right, as most of the late-comers understand, then it would be expected that this cure should occur for other blind people who seek to do *tawassul* by the status of the Prophet (ﷺ), and sometimes they add to that the status of all the prophets and messengers, and all of the *awliyaa*, the martyrs and the pious, and the status of all those who have any status before Allaah, those from all the angels, men and *jinn*! We do not know, and we do not think that anyone knows it to have worked for anyone in all these long centuries after the death of the Prophet(ﷺ) till today.

So if it is clear to the noble reader from the various proofs we have shown that the *hadeeth* of the blind man revolves around *tawassul* by his (ﷺ) *du'aa* and that it has no connection to *tawassul* by his person, then it becomes clear that the saying of the blind man in his *du'aa*, "O Allaah I ask You and turn to You by means of Your Prophet Muhammad (ﷺ)," means 'I seek a means of nearness to You by means of the *du'aa* of Your Prophet (ﷺ),' with the governing word [i.e. *du'aa*] omitted, and this is something well known in the language, as in Allaah, the Most High's, Saying:

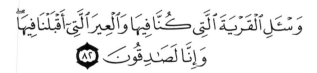

"And ask the town where we have been, and the caravans in which we returned, and indeed we are telling the truth."[91]

---

91. Soorah Yoosuf (12): 82

Meaning "The people" of the town and "the companions"[92] of the caravan, and we and the opponents agree upon that, i.e. that we have to come up with the governing word which has been omitted. In our view it is the same case as with the *du'aa* of 'Umar, *radiyallaahu 'anhu*, and his *tawassul* by means of al-Abbaas, *radiyallaahu 'anhu*, either it should be taken to be, "I turn to You by means of the (status) of Your Prophet," and "O Muhammad I turn by your (person) or your (position) to my Lord," as they claim, or, "I turn to You by means of the (*du'aa*) of Your Prophet," and "O Muhammad I turn by your (*du'aa*) to my Lord," which is our saying.

One of these two possibilities has to be accepted and preferred due to an evidence which proves its correctness. So as for their saying that the missing governing word is 'status/position' then they have no proof for it, neither in this nor in any other *hadeeth*, since there is nothing mentioned along with it which suggests or states any mention of 'status' or indicates it at all. Just as they have nothing from the Quraan or the *Sunnah*, or from the practice of the Companions where there is *tawassul* by anyone's status. So this preferred view of theirs has nothing to support it and so is rendered baseless and not given any further consideration. As regards our saying then it is supported by many proofs which have preceded.

There is something else which should be mentioned. If the *hadeeth* of the blind man was taken to have its apparent meaning, which is *tawassul* by his person then it would clash with and nullify his saying which follows, *O Allaah accept his shafaa'ah on my behalf and accept my shafaa'ah for him*, and this is not permissible as is obvious. So it is binding to harmonise between the first and the last sentences and there is no way to do this except in the way that we have shown, i.e. that the *tawassul* was by means of *du'aa*. So this is established and its use as a proof for *tawassul* by his person is invalidated, and all praise is for Allaah.

---

92. Even though these words are omitted.

Even if it were correct that the blind man sought to make *tawassul* by his (ﷺ) person, then it would be something particular for him (ﷺ), not something shared by the rest of the prophets and the pious, and joining them in it along with him is not something acceptable, since he (ﷺ) was the leader and most noble of them all. So it could have been something which Allaah particularised him with, like many other things reported in authentic narrations, and the matters of particularised qualities are not within the scope of analogy. So he thinks that the blind man's *tawassul* to Allaah was by means of his (ﷺ) person, then he should halt at that and not add others to it, as is reported from Imaam Ahmad and ash-Shaikh al-'Izz ibn 'Abdis-Salaam, *rahimahullaahu.*

This is what scholarly research and justice demands, and it is Allaah who guides to and grants attainment of what is correct.

REMOVAL OF A MISUNDERSTANDING

Following this it is essential that we explain a very important point relating to this topic and that is that when we deny *tawassul* by means of the status of the Prophet (ﷺ) and the status of others from the prophets and the pious, then that is not because we deny that they have high status, esteem and position with Allaah, nor is it due to hatred of them or because our hearts do not have great love of them, which we are falsely accused of by Dr. Bootee in his book: *Fiqhus-Seerah* (p.354), where he said: "Some people have gone astray, those whose hearts do not have love of Allaah's Messenger (ﷺ), so they deny *tawassul* by means of his (ﷺ) person after his death..." Indeed no, not at all. Rather we are, and all praise and thanks are for Allaah, amongst those who give great esteem to Allaah's Messenger(ﷺ) and have the most love for him, and recognise his excellence. Rather if this person's saying indicates anything, then it merely shows the blind malice which fills the hearts of the enemies of the *Salafee da'wah* and the hatred which they have for this *da'wah* and its people, even to the point that it leads them to this very dangerous and bigoted position. It leads them to commit this repugnant and abominable crime, to devour the flesh of their brother Muslims and to declare them to be Unbelievers without a proof, except for suspicion which is the worst of false speech, as was said by the noblest Prophet (ﷺ).[93]

So I do not know how this person who oppresses his own soul allows himself to pass this ruling which cannot be given except by Allaah, the Mighty and Majestic, the One who alone knows all the secrets of the hearts and what is hidden in the chests. Do you think that he does not know the penalty awaiting one who does that, or is it that he knows it, however his hatred and hidden malice for the callers of the *Sunnah* blind him to it? Whichever of the two it is, we remind him of these two noble *hadeeth* that perhaps he will withdraw from his error, awaken from his foolhardy heedlessness, and repent from his actions.

Allaah's Messenger (ﷺ) said: *Whichever man declares a Muslim man to be an Unbeliever, then either he is indeed an Unbeliever or he himself* (i.e. the one who says it) *is the Unbeliever.*[94]

He (ﷺ) said: *One of the worst forms of usury (ribaa) is falsely accusing the honour of a Muslim.*[95]

Then finally we say to him: Do you not realise that by saying these words you are rebutting the Pious Predecessors of this *Ummah* and declaring as Unbelievers its *mujtahid imaams*, who do not allow intercession by means of the Prophet (ﷺ) or anyone else after is death. Amongst them Aboo Haneefah and his companions, *rahimahullaah*, and Aboo Haneefah said: "I hate that

---

93. Reported by al-Bukhaaree (translation 8/53/no.90) and Muslim (translation 1361/4/no.6214).

94. Reported by al-Bukhaaree (translation 8/80/no.125) and Muslim (translation 1/41/no.116) from Aboo Hurairah, *radiyallaahu 'anhu*, and others.

95. Reported by Ahmad and Aboo Daawood (3/1359/no.4858) from Sa'eed ibn Zayd and its *isnaad* is *saheeh*.

anyone should seek *tawassul* to Allaah except by means of Allaah" as has preceded.

'So if you do not know then that is a misfortune, but if you know then the misfortune is even greater.'

We repeat and say that every sincere and just person will know for certain that we, and all praise and thanks are for Allaah, are amongst those who have the greatest love for Allaah's Messenger (ﷺ) and from those who most respect his (ﷺ) position, rights and excellence, and that he is the most excellent of the Prophets, noblest of the Messengers, the last and best of them, the companion of the banner of praise, the Pond/Lake (*al-Hawd*), the Greater Intercession, the singular position of excellence, the clear miracles, and that Allaah, the Most High, abrogated every previous religion with his religion, and sent down the seven oft-repeated *Aayaat* and the Sublime Quraan upon him, and made his nation the best nation brought for the people, to the end of all his (ﷺ) excellent qualities and virtues which clearly show his great standing and high status, may Allaah shower praises and blessings of complete peace upon him and his family and true followers.

All praise and thanks are for Allaah, we are amongst the first of the people to affirm all of that, and perhaps his (ﷺ) status is more safely guarded by far, with us than with the others who claim to love him and make a show of recognising his position.

However what counts here is only true following of him (ﷺ), compliance to his orders, and avoidance of what he forbade. As Allaah, the One free of all defect and blemish and the Most High, says:

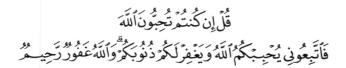

"Say (O Muhammad (ﷺ) to mankind): 'If you love Allaah then follow me, Allaah will love you and forgive you your sins.'"[96]

By the grace of Allaah we are the keenest of people in obedience to Allaah, the Mighty and Majestic, and in following His Prophet (ﷺ), and these are the two truest proofs of sincere love and regard, as opposed to exaggerated veneration and going beyond bounds in praise of someone, both of which have been forbidden by Allaah, the Most High, He, the One free of all blemish and defect, says:

$$ يَٰٓأَهۡلَ ٱلۡكِتَٰبِ لَا تَغۡلُواْ فِى دِينِكُمۡ وَلَا تَقُولُواْ عَلَى ٱللَّهِ إِلَّا ٱلۡحَقَّ $$

"O people of Scripture (Jews and Christians)! Do not exceed the limits in your religion, nor say of Allaah aught but the truth."[97]

Likewise the Prophet (ﷺ) forbade them, saying: *Do not exaggerate in praising me as the Christians exaggerated in their praise if Ibn Maryam (Jesus). For indeed I am a Slave, so say 'The Slave of Allaah and His Messenger'.*[98]

It is fitting that we mention that the Prophet (ﷺ) declared that from exceeding the limits in religion is that the person making *Hajj* when stoning the pillars in Minaa should do so with large pebbles, rather he ordered that they should be slightly longer than chick-peas. From Ibn 'Abbaas, *radiyallaahu 'anhumaa*, who said: Allaah's Messenger (ﷺ) said to me on the morning of *al-'Aqabah*: *Give me small pebbles for the stoning*. He said: So I sought for

---

96. Soorah Aali-'Imraan (3): 31
97. Soorah An-Nisaa (4): 171
98. Reported by al-Bukhaaree (translation 4/435/no.654) and others.

pebbles the size of largish chick-peas, then when I put them in his hand he said: *The like of these* (three times) *and beware of exceeding the limits in religion, since those who came before you were destroyed due to exceeding the limits in religion.*[99]

This was because he counted stoning the pillars amongst the symbolic actions, whose goal was the disavowal of and to fight against Satan, not to actually kill him thereby. So the Muslim here should carry out the order and disavow and reject Satan, the moral enemy of mankind, showing enmity to him, just this. Then despite this severe warning against exceeding the limits in the religion, the Muslims have unfortunately fallen into it and have followed the ways of the people of the Book. One of them said:

> "Leave aside what the Christians claim about their Prophet -
> But deliver whatever other praise you wish upon him
> [Muhammad (ﷺ)] and do so as you yourself decide."

This poet is held in high esteem by many of the Muslims, who often chant this poem of his which is well known as *al-Burdah*, and they seek to use it as a blessing; they sing it on birthday celebrations which they hold, and in some gatherings of admonition or knowledge; because they think that this is something which draws them closer to Allaah, the Blessed and Most High, and that it is a proof of their love for their Prophet (ﷺ). This poet thinks that the forbiddance reported in the previous *hadeeth* is merely a prevention of claiming that Muhammad (ﷺ) is the son of Allaah, so he prohibits this particular saying, but he calls to any other saying whatever it may be. This is a serious error and clear misguidance since the excessive praise which is forbidden in the *hadeeth* has two meanings. The first of these is unrestricted praise, and the second is praise which goes beyond the limits. So upon this it may be that the

---

99. Reported by Ahmad (1/215 and 347), an-Nasaa'ee, Ibn Maajah and others. It is found in my book *as-Saheehah* (no.1283) and *Takhreej as-Sunnah Li-Ibn Abee 'Aasim* (no.98).

forbidding *hadeeth* means a forbiddance of praising him (ﷺ), in order to prevent going beyond bounds, and sufficing with the fact that Allaah, the Most High, chose him as a Prophet and a Messenger, and as His beloved and chosen one, and with what He praised him with in His Saying:

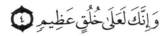

"And verily, you (O Muhammad) are on an exalted standard of character."[100]

Since what is it possible for any human to say about him after this Saying of Allaah, the Blessed and Most High? What worth will any words which they say carry before this witness of Allaah, the Most High? Indeed the greatest praise we can give to him (ﷺ) is that we say about him what our Lord, the Mighty and Majestic, said: that he is His Slave and His Messenger. That is the greatest possible attestation in his (ﷺ) favour and it contains no element of going beyond bounds, nor of neglect of his due rights and honour. So our Lord, the One free of all defects and blemish, described him when he was at the highest station and position of honour given to him by Allaah, the Most High, and that was when He took him on the Night Journey and caused him to ascend to the highest heavens, and showed him the greatest signs of his Lord, at this point he described him with the attribute of his being a slave/worshipper, Saying:

سُبْحَٰنَ ٱلَّذِىٓ أَسْرَىٰ بِعَبْدِهِۦ لَيْلًا مِّنَ ٱلْمَسْجِدِ ٱلْحَرَامِ
إِلَى ٱلْمَسْجِدِ ٱلْأَقْصَا

"Glorified (and Exalted) be He (Allaah) [above all that they associate with Him]. Who took His *slave/worshipper* (Muhammad) for a journey by night from *Al-Masjid*

---

100. Soorah Al-Qalam (68): 4

al-Haraam (*Makkah*) to the Farthest Mosque (in Jerusalem)."[101]

It is also possible that the meaning (of the *hadeeth*) is: Do not go to extremes in praising me, so that you praise me with things which are not right for me, and that you attribute to me some of the things which are particular to Allaah, the Blessed and the Most High.

Perhaps the most correct meaning is the first due to two matters:

(i) The completion of the *hadeeth* which is his (ﷺ) saying: *So say: The Slave of Allaah and His Messenger*. Meaning: suffice with the description that Allaah, the Blessed and the Most High, has given to me, that He has chosen me as His Slave/Worshipper and His Messenger.

(ii) The chapter heading that some of the scholars provide for this *hadeeth*. So for example, Imaam at-Tirmidhee places it under the heading: "Modesty of the Prophet (ﷺ)." So he takes the *hadeeth* to be a forbiddance of praise, since that is what is consistent with the meaning of modesty and is in harmony with it.

ADDITIONS TO THE HADEETH OF THE BLIND MAN

It should be known that in other narrations of the previous *hadeeth* of the blind man there occur two additions whose weakness and contradiction to what is authentic must be explained, so that the reader is clear about them and will not be deceived by the saying of those who use them as a proof to oppose what is true and correct.

The first addition

The addition of Hammaad ibn Salamah who said that Aboo Ja'far al-Khatamee narrated to us: ..., and he quotes its chain of narration as in the narration of

---

101. Soorah Al-Israa (17): 1

Shu'bah, and likewise the text except that he abridged it slightly and added at the end after his saying: "And my Prophet supplicated on my behalf for my sight to be restored." He added: "And if you have a need then do the same." It is reported by Aboo Bakr ibn Abee Khaithamah in his *Tareekh*, and he says: "Muslim ibn Ibraaheem narrated to us, Hammaad ibn Salamah narrated to us..."

This addition has been declared weak by Shaikhul-Islaam Ibn Taimiyyah in *al-Qaa'idatul-Jaliyyah* (p.102) due to its being reported by Hammaad ibn Salamah alone, and the fact that he contradicts the narration of Shu'bah who is the soundest narrator who reports this *hadeeth*. This declaration of weakness for this reason is indeed in full agreement with the principles of the science of *hadeeth* and in no way contradicts them. As for the saying of al-Ghumaaree in *al-Misbah* (p.30) that Hammaad is reliable, and is a narrator depended upon by the authors of the *saheeh*, and that the addition of a reliable narrator is acceptable, then this is either an oversight due to negligence or a pretence of such with regard to the science of *hadeeth*. This is because such acceptance is conditional upon the fact that the narrator does not contradict one who is more reliable than himself. Al-Haafidh says in *Nukhbatul-Fikr*: "And an addition is acceptable as long as it is not contradicting one who is more reliable. If it is contradicted by that which is more reliable, then that which is reliable is what is declared correct and preserved (*mahfoodh*) and the other is declared weak due to its contradiction of that which is more reliable (*shaadh*)."

This condition is not found here since Hammaad ibn Salamah, even though he is one of the narrators used by Muslim, yet still without a doubt he is below the station of Shu'bah in memorisation and preservation. This fact will become clear to you if you refer to the biographies of both of them in the source works. The first of them is mentioned by adh-Dhahabee in *al-Meezaan*, and he only mentions in it those against whom criticism has been levelled, and he describes him as "Reliable but commits errors," whereas he does not mention

Shu'bah in that book at all. The difference between them will also be seen by carefully considering the biography which al-Haafidh [Ibn Hajr] provides for each of them. He says in *at-Taqreeb*: "Hammaad ibn Salamah: Reliable, a worshipper, the most reliable narrator from Thaabit, and his memory deteriorated in later life," and he says: "Shu'bah ibn al-Hajjaj: Reliable, foremost memoriser, precise; ath-Thawree used to say: 'He is the chief of the believers with regard to *Hadeeth*,' and he was the first of the people of 'Iraq to investigate the veracity of narrators; he defended the *Sunnah* and was a worshipper." When this is clear to you then you will know that the contradiction of Hammaad to the narration of Shu'bah in this *hadeeth* means that this addition is not acceptable, since it is a contradiction of the narration of one who is more reliable, and is therefore *shaadh* (weak narration contradicting what is more reliable), as is seen from the words of al-Haafidh previously quoted from *Nukhbatul-Fikr*. It may also be that Hammaad narrated this *hadeeth* after his memory deteriorated and he fell into errors. It is as if Imaam Ahmad indicates the weakness of this addition since he reports the *hadeeth* by way of Muammal (who is Ibn Ismaa'eel), from Hammaad, after the previous narration of Shu'bah, but he does not quote the wording of the *hadeeth* (with the addition), rather, he refers it back to the wording of the *hadeeth* of Shu'bah and says: "And he mentioned the *hadeeth*." It is also a possibility that the addition is not found in the narration of Muammal from Hammaad, which would also explain why Imaam Ahmad did not mention it, since the practice of the scholars and memorisers when they refer such a narration back to its wording which has preceded is that they also mention any additional wording not found in the first narration. So in conclusion the additional wording is not authentic due to its being *Shaadh* (contradicting a more reliable narration).

Even if it were authentic it would not be a proof for the permissibility of *tawassul* by means of his (ﷺ) person since his saying: "Then do the same" could mean: come again to the Prophet (ﷺ) in his lifetime and ask him to supplicate and make that a means of *tawassul*, and make *wudoo*, and pray, and then recite the supplication which the Messenger of Allaah (ﷺ) taught him to supplicate with, and Allaah knows best.

The second addition

The story of the man who came to 'Uthmaan ibn 'Affaan and used the Prophet (ﷺ) as a means of *tawassul* in order for his need to be fulfilled. It is reported by at-Tabaraanee in *al-Mu'jamus-Sagheer* (pp.103-104) and in *al-Kabeer* (3/2/1/1-2) by way of 'Abdullaah ibn Wahb, from Shabeeb ibn Sa'eed al-Makkee, from Rawh ibn al-Qaasim, from Aboo Ja'far al-Khatamee al-Madanee, from Aboo Umaamah ibn Sahl ibn Haneef, from his paternal uncle 'Uthmaan ibn Haneef: "That a man used to go to 'Uthmaan ibn 'Affaan, *radiyallaahu 'anhu*, for some need which he had, and 'Uthmaan had not used to take any notice of him and would not fulfil his need, so he met 'Uthmaan ibn Haneef and complained to him about it, so 'Uthmaan said to him: "Go to the place of *wudoo*, make *wudoo*, then come to the mosque and pray two *rak'ahs* in it and then say: 'O Allaah I ask You and turn to You by means of Your Prophet Muhammad (ﷺ), the Prophet of mercy, O Muhammad I turn by means of you to your Lord, the Mighty and Majestic, so that He should fulfil my need for me,' and you should mention your need, then return to me so that I should go off with you. So the man went off and did as he said, them came to the door of 'Uthmaan ibn 'Affaan, *radiyallaahu 'anhu*. So the door keeper came and took his hand and entered him and sat him upon the mat along with him ('Uthmaan ibn 'Affaan). He said to him: "What is your need." So he mentioned it to him and he carried it out for him, then he said to him: "I have not remembered your need until now," and he said: "Whenever you have a need then come to us." Then the man left him and met 'Uthmaan ibn Haneef and said to him: "May Allaah reward you with good, he had not used to pay any attention to my need nor take any notice of me until you spoke to him about it." So 'Uthmaan ibn Haneef said: "By Allaah, I have not spoken to him, but I witnessed the incident when a blind man came to the Allaah's Messenger (ﷺ) and he complained to him about the loss of his sight. So the Prophet (ﷺ) said to him that he should have patience, so he said: "O Messenger of Allaah I have no one to lead me around." So the Prophet (ﷺ) said: *Go to the place of wudoo, make*

wudoo, then pray two rak'aks, then supplicate with these supplications."
'Uthmaan ibn Haneef said: By Allaah we did not depart, and we spoke for a
long time, until the man re-entered upon us and it was as if there had never
been anything wrong with his eyes."

At-Tabaraanee said: "No one reports it from Rawh ibn al-Qaasim except
Shabeeb ibn Sa'eed, Aboo Sa'eed al-Makkee and he is reliable. He is also the
one whom Ahmad ibn Shabeeb narrates from, narrating from his father, from
Yoonus ibn Yazeed al-Aylee. This *hadeeth* is also reported from Shu'bah from
Aboo Ja'far al-Khatamee, whose name is 'Umayr ibn Yazeed, and he is reliable.
It is reported from Shu'bah only by 'Uthmaan ibn 'Umar ibn Faaris, and the
hadeeth is *Saheeh*."

There is no doubt about the authenticity of the *hadeeth*, but rather what needs
to be checked here is this story which is reported only by Shabeeb ibn Sa'eed
as pointed out by at-Tabaraanee. Indeed this narrator Shabeeb has been criticised, particularly with regard to what Ibn Wahb narrates from him. Then we
find here that there are also others who narrate from him: Ismaa'eel and
Ahmad, the two sons of the aforementioned Shabeeb ibn Sa'eed. As for
Ismaa'eel, then I do not know him and I do not find anyone who mentions
him. Indeed they neglect him to the point that they do not even mention him
amongst those who narrate from his father, as opposed to his brother Ahmad
since he is *sadooq* (generally acceptable). As for his father Shabeeb then what
they say about him is, in conclusion, that he was reliable, yet having weakness
in his memory, except for those narrations reported from him by his son
Ahmad which he himself reports from Yoonus in particular in which case he is
a proof. Adh-Dhahabee said in *al-Meezaan*: "*Sadooq* (generally acceptable)
who makes errors, Ibn 'Adiyy mentions him in his *Kaamil* and said: "He has a
written manuscript copy of *hadeeth* from Yoonus ibn Yazeed which is fine. Ibn
Wahb reports some weak and reprehensible things from him. Ibnul-Madeenee
said: He used to go to Egypt for trade and his written narrations are reliable
and are written down from him by his son Ahmad." Ibn 'Adiyy said: "Shabeeb

sometimes made slips and errors when he narrated from memory. I hope that he did not do this intentionally. Then when his son Ahmad narrates from him with the *ahaadeeth* of Yoonus, then it is as if it is a different Yoonus, meaning: he makes them good." So this speech means that the *ahaadeeth* of this narrator Shabeeb are all right with two conditions:

(i) That they are narrated from him by his son Ahmad, and

(ii) That Shabeeb is narrating from Yoonus. The reason being that he possessed the written manuscript of Yoonus ibn Yazeed, as Ibn Abee Haatim says in *al-Jarh wat-Ta'deel*, from his father (2/1/359), so when he narrates from his books then he narrates well, but when he narrates from his memory he makes mistakes as Ibn 'Adiyy says.

Therefore the saying of al-Haafidh in his biography in *at-Taqreeb*: "His *ahaadeeth* are all right when they are narrated from him by his son Ahmad, but not when narrated from him by Ibn Wahb," is deficient, since it gives the impression that all the narrations of his son Ahmad from him are acceptable. This is however not the case. Rather this is conditional on the fact that they are *ahaadeeth* which he himself narrates from Yoonus, as has preceded. This is further evidenced by the fact that al-Haafidh himself has elsewhere indicated this condition. Indeed he mentions Shabeeb amongst those narrators used by al-Bukhaaree who have been criticised, found in the introduction of *Fathul-Baaree* (p.133), then he rejects this criticism, after having quoted those who declare him reliable and mentioning the saying of Ibn 'Adiyy about him, saying: "I say: al-Bukhaaree brings his *ahaadeeth* which were reported from him by his son, which he himself reports from Yoonus, but he does not bring anything which he himself reports from other than Yoonus, and he does not quote anything which Ibn Wahb reports from him." So here he, *rahimahullaah*, gives an indication that criticism is valid about Shabeeb when he is reporting from other than Yoonus, even if they are things which his son Ahmad reports from him. This is what is correct as we have just explained, and in light of it we should understand what he says in *at-Taqreeb* in order to harmonise between his words and to avoid creating contradictions.

So when this is clear the weakness of this story will be manifest, and the lack of its suitability as a proof. Then a further weakness is apparent to me in it, and it is the presence of conflicting reports from Ahmad ibn Shabeeb. The *hadeeth* is also reported by Ibn as-Sunnee in *'Amalul-Yawm wal-Laylah* (p.202) and by al-Haakim (1/526) by way of three chains from Ahmad ibn Shabeeb without any mention of the attached story. It is likewise reported by 'Awn ibn 'Umaarah al-Basree: Rawh ibn al-Qaasim narrated to us with it. This is reported by al-Haakim. Then even though this narrator 'Awn is weak, yet still his narration is to be given precedence over the narration of Shabeeb because he is agreed with in it by Shu'bah and Hammaad ibn Salamah, from Aboo Ja'far al-Khatamee.[102]

So in conclusion this story is weak and contrary to what is authentically reported due to three reasons:

(i) The weakness of the memory of the one who is alone in reporting it;
(ii) and the conflicting reports from him and;
(iii) his contradicting those reliable narrators who do not mention it in the *hadeeth*.

A single one of these reasons would be sufficient to negate this story, so how about when all three are found together?

One of the strange examples of blind bigotry and following of desires is that Shaikh al-Ghumaaree quotes the various narrations of this story in *al-Misbah* (p.12&17) by way of al-Bayhaqee in *ad-Dalaa'il*, and at-Tabaraanee, and then does not say anything at all about their authenticity or weakness. The reason

---

102. Translator's note: i.e. none of them report the additional story involving 'Uthmaan ibn 'Affaan.

for this is clear: As for a declaration of their authenticity, then it cannot be possible according to the science of *hadeeth*, and as for a declaration of their weakness, then that is the truth... The like is committed by one deprived of correctness in *al-Isaabah* (pp.21-22) who quotes the *hadeeth* along with this story and then they say: "And this *hadeeth* is declared authentic by at-Tabaraanee in *as-Sagheer* and *al-Kabeer*"?! But this saying despite its brevity contains a number of points of ignorance:

(i) At-Tabaraanee does not declare this *hadeeth* to be authentic in *al-Kabeer* but rather in *as-Sagheer* only. I quoted the *hadeeth* for the readers directly from his book, not taking it from an intermediary source as these people who have only a very limited share of this noble knowledge do. "And whoever takes water from the ocean will fill the irrigation canals."

(ii) At-Tabaraanee only declared the *hadeeth* authentic, not the story as is shown by his saying, as has preceded: "And the *hadeeth* has been reported by Shu'bah .. and the *hadeeth* is authentic." So this is a clear statement that what he was talking about was the same *hadeeth* as that reported by Shu'bah, and Shu'bah did not narrate the story, so at-Tabaraanee did not declare that to be authentic, so there is no proof for them in his words.

(iii) Even if that story were authentic from 'Uthmaan ibn Haneef, then in it he did not teach the full supplication to the blind man. Rather he dropped the sentence: "O Allaah accept his *shafaa'ah* for me, (i.e. accept him as a supplicant for me), and accept my *shafaa'ah* for him (i.e. accept my supplication for his to be accepted)." since he would have understood, with his pure Arabian disposition, that this saying would necessitate that the Prophet (ﷺ) should supplicate for this man, just as he supplicated for the blind man. Then since this was not possible with regard for that man he did not mention that sentence. Shaikhul-Islaam Ibn Taymiyyah said (p.104): "And as is known if a person after his (ﷺ) death were to say: 'O Allaah accept him as a supplicant for me, and accept my supplication for his to be answered,' despite the fact that the Prophet (ﷺ) did not supplicate for him, then this saying of the person would be a futile saying. 'Uthmaan ibn Haneef did not order him to ask the

Prophet (ﷺ) for anything, nor did he tell him to say "Accept him as a supplicant for me," nor did he order him to make the full supplication, rather he ordered him with a part of it. There was to be no supplication on his behalf from the Prophet (ﷺ) nor anything which could be imagined as such, so if one were to say after his death: "Then accept him as a supplicant for me" then it would be a meaningless saying. Therefore 'Uthmaan did not order it, nor did he order the supplication as it was ordered by the Prophet (ﷺ). Further what he ordered was something not reported from the Prophet (ﷺ), and the like of this cannot be used to establish something in the *Sharee'ah*, just like everything else that is only as the view of a single Companion, whether with regard to excellence of certain acts of worship, permitted acts, obligatory acts, or forbidden acts, when their saying does not find the support of other Companions, and that which is reported from the Prophet (ﷺ) is either contrary to it, or at least does not affirm it. Then in such a case his action does not become part of the *Sunnah* which must be followed by the Muslims. Rather the most that can be said about it is that it is a matter where personal deduction of the people of knowledge (*ijtihaad*) can be employed, and a matter about which the *Ummah* have disagreed, so it must be referred back to Allaah and His Messenger."

Then he mentions many examples of things which were the view of individual Companions and which they are not followed upon, for example Ibn 'Umar's entering water beneath his eyelids whilst making *wudoo* and so on, so refer to that. Then he said: "Then if that is the case, then as is known, if it were established from 'Uthmaan ibn Haneef or someone else that he declared as being prescribed or recommended that a person should seek *tawassul* by means of the Prophet (ﷺ) after his death, without the Prophet (ﷺ) supplicating for him, nor interceding in that for him, then we know that 'Umar and the greater Companions did not hold that to be prescribed after his death as it was prescribed in his lifetime. Rather during his lifetime they used to seek *tawassul* by means of the Prophet (ﷺ) when praying for rain in his lifetime, but after he died they did not seek *tawassul* by means of him. Rather 'Umar said in the supplication which is authentically reported and famous from him, established by agreement of the scholars, and it was done in the famous year of drought and destruction in the presence of the Muhaajiroon and the Ansaar, when the drought became so severe that 'Umar swore that fat was not to be eaten until produce returned. Then he prayed for rain for the people and said: "O Allaah when we used to suffer drought we used to use our Prophet as a means of nearness to You and You would grant us rain, now we seek nearness to You by means of the uncle of our Prophet, so grant us rain," and they would be blessed with rain. Then this supplication was agreed to by all the Companions present, and none of them criticised it and it was well-known. So this is one of the clearest cases of tacit consensus (*ijmaa'*). Then a similar supplication was made by Mu'aawiyah ibn Abee Sufyaan during his *Khilaafah*, and if seeking *tawassul* by means of the Prophet (ﷺ) after his death was just like seeking *tawassul* by means of him in his lifetime, then they would have said: "How can we seek *tawassul* by means of al-'Abbaas and Yazeed ibn al-Aswad and their like, and abandon *tawassul* by means of the Prophet (ﷺ) who is the best of creation and the best and greatest means of *tawassul* with Allaah?" Since not a single one of them said that, and we know that in his lifetime they sought *tawasssul* by means of his supplication on behalf of the people, and that after his death they sought *tawassul* by means of the supplication of others, then we know that what was prescribed with them was to seek *tawassul* by means of the person's supplication, not by means of his person."

Furthermore there is a sentence in the story which if an intelligent and wise person who knows about the virtues of the Companions was to consider he would find it a further proof of the weakness and incorrectness of the story. It is the saying that the rightly-guided *Caliph* 'Uthmaan, *radiyallaahu 'anhu*, had not used to take any notice of that mans need and would ignore it! So how does this agree with what is authentically reported from the Prophet (ﷺ) that the angels used to feel shy from 'Uthmaan, and with what is well-known about him, *radiyallaahu 'anhu*, that he used to treat the people with kindness, gentleness and goodness? All of this causes us to further doubt that this story took place, since it shows oppression which totally conflicts with his behaviour and manner, *radiyallaahu 'anhu*.

NOTE: After having written what was necessary here we came across a book: *At-Tawassul ilaa Haqeeqatit-Tawassul* by Shaikh Muhammad Naseebur-Rifaa'ee, who adds to his name the title: "Founder and servant of the *Salafee daw'ah...*" So scholarly honesty and sincerity, and the obligation of offering sincere advice and the necessity of speaking the truth demands that we make Allaah's judgement clear as we understand it, and explain what we hold as religion before Allaah, the Most High, with regard to that title. We should make clear that the *Salafee da'wah* is only the true call of *Islaam*, just as Allaah, the Most High, sent it down upon the last of His Messengers and Prophets, Muhammad (ﷺ). So Allaah alone, the One free of any defect or blemish, is its founder and originator, and no human no matter who he is can claim to be its founder and originator. Even the noblest Prophet (ﷺ), his role was to faithfully accept and retain, and to convey completely with full precision, and it was not permitted for him to make any alteration to anything which Allaah, the Most High, prescribed and revealed. Therefore for any person, no matter how high in station, to claim to have founded this divine and blessed *da'wah* has in reality made a very great mistake and a serious fault, that is if it is not a case of major *shirk*, and we seek the refuge of Allaah, the Most High. So we do not know how this was fallen into by a man who lived for a long time with his brothers in Aleppo and other places in Syria upon the *Salafee da'wah*, which has as one of its most particular characteristics and gives the greatest importance to fighting *shirk* and idolatry in wordings, not to mention *shirk* in matters of *'aqeedah*. This brother then separated himself and this dangerous deviation was one of the results of leaving the united body of Believers upon the truth. May Allaah, the Most High, guide us and him, and keep us away from errors, trials and desires which lead people astray. Perhaps someone will try to find an excuse for the author by saying that what he meant by that title was that he was the reviver of the *Salafee Da'wah*, not that he was its originator and founder of its teachings, and that there were indeed revivers of the religion in earlier and later times, and perhaps the author thinks that he is one of them.

Yes indeed there were revivers of the call to true *Islaam* in successive ages, but what a difference there is between this author and those revivers, and it would be sufficient for him to have been a follower of one of them. Even if we were to agree to his placing himself amongst them, then it would still be necessary for him to quote the limits of his claimed status as a reviver, such as his limiting that to a certain land or area. However his use of that title unrestrictedly in its widest sense gives the impression to the readers that he is the reviver of *Islaam* for the whole Islamic world today, and how can he claim that?

From the basic manners which the Muslim caller must have is modesty, and being far from love of fame, boasting and making claims for oneself. These things are fatal maladies which strip the one who strives for them and craves after them of competence to give *da'wah*. They divest him of his most effective weapon against his enemies and cause his actions to be rendered void and futile, and we seek Allaah's refuge, and we ask Allaah to protect and guide us.

We quickly examined the aforementioned book and found some errors in it, some of which we will indicate where fitting. From these is that he says on p.237 whilst talking about the chain of narration of the previous story: "In the chain of narration of this story there is a man whose name is Rawh ibn Salaah and he was declared to be weak by the majority and by Ibn 'Adiyy, and Ibn Yoonus said: He reports weak *ahaadeeth* which contradict what is authentic." This is a total error and we do not know how he fell into it, since this person, Rawh ibn Saalih, is the cause of weakness of the third *hadeeth* which will follow.

• *the third doubt*
WEAK *AHAADEETH* RELATING TO *TAWASSUL*

Those who seek to permit innovated forms of *tawassul* use many *ahaadeeth* as evidence, but when we consider them we find that they fall into two categories:

(i) Those which are authentic from the Prophet (ﷺ) but do not show what these people claim, nor support their view. For example the *hadeeth* of the blind man, and we have already spoken about this category.

(ii) Those which are not authentic from Allaah's Messenger (ﷺ), some of them showing what they hold and others which do not indicate that. These inauthentic *ahaadeeth* are many and we shall suffice with mentioning those which are well-known.

First Hadeeth : From Aboo Sa'eed al-Khudree, quoted as the saying of the Prophet (ﷺ): "Whoever goes out from his house for the prayer and says: 'O Allaah, I ask You by the right of those who ask of You, and I ask You by the right of this walking of mine, since I do not go out for wickedness or pride...,' then Allaah turns His Face to him." It is reported by Ahmad (3/21) and the wording is his, and Ibn Maajah, and it can be found fully referenced in *Silsilatul-Ahaadeeth id-Da'eefah* (no.24), and its chain of narration is weak since it is narrated through 'Atiyyah al-'Awfee from Aboo Sa'eed al-Khudree. 'Atiyyah is weak as declared by an-Nawawee in *al-Adhkaar*, Ibn Taimiyyah in *al-Qaa'idatul-Jaliyyah* and adh-Dhahabee in *al-Meezaan*; indeed in *ad-Du'afaa* (88/1) he says: "They are agreed upon his weakness." Also by al-Haafidh al-Haithamee in various places in *Majma'uz-Zawaa'id* from them (5/236). He is also mentioned by Aboo Bakr ibn al-Muhibb al-Ba'labakee in *ad-Du'afaa wal-Matrookeen*, and by al-Boosayree as will follow. Likewise al-Haafidh Ibn Hajr says of him: "Truthful but makes many mistakes; he was a *Shee'ee mudallis*." So he clarifies this narrator's weakness and it is due to two things: (i) The weakness of his memory as shown by his saying: "He makes many mistakes." This is like his saying about him in *Tabaqaatul-Mudalliseen*: "weak in *hadeeth*." Even more clear is his saying about him in *"Talkheesul-Habeer* (p.241, Indian edn.) whilst discussing another *hadeeth*: "It contains 'Atiyyah ibn Sa'eed al-'Awfee and he is weak." (ii) His *tadlees*. However al-Haafidh should have explained the type of *tadlees* which he performed, since *tadlees* with the scholars of *hadeeth* is of many types, the most well-known of which are:

(a) That a narrator reports a narration from someone he met when in fact he did not directly hear that narration from him, or that he narrated something from a contemporary whom he did not actually meet, giving the impression that he heard it from him. For example by saying 'From so and so' or 'so and so said.'

(b) That the narrator calls his Shaikh by an unfamiliar name or title, different to the name by which he is commonly known in order to hide his true identity. The scholars have clearly stated that this is something forbidden if his Shaikh was an unreliable narrator, and he does this to hide his identity or to give the impression that he was a different reliable narrator with the same name or title.[103] This is known as *tadleesush-Shuyookh*.

The *tadlees* of 'Atiyyah was of this forbidden type as I have explained in my book: *Silsilatul-Ahaadeethid-Da'eefah* (no.24).

So in conclusion we say that 'Atiyyah used to narrate from Aboo Sa'eed al-Khudree, *radiyallaahu 'anhu*, then when he died he used to sit with one of the great liars well known for lying about *hadeeth*, who was al-Kalbee. Then 'Atiyyah used to narrate from him, but when doing so would call him 'Aboo Sa'eed' to give the impression to those listening that he had heard these narrations from Aboo Sa'eed al-Khudree! This to me in itself would be enough to destroy the credibility of 'Atiyyah, so how about when we have in addition to it his weak memory! Therefore I would have been pleased for al-Haafidh to clarify the fact that it was this evil type of *tadlees* which 'Atiyyah was guilty of, even if only by an indication as he does in *Tabaqaatul-Mudalliseen* by his saying: "Well-known for evil *tadlees*," as has preceded. It is as if al-Haafidh forgot

---

103. *Ikhtisaar 'Uloomil-Hadeeth* of Ibn Katheer (p.59) with the explanation of Ahmad Shaakir.

or erred, or something else, as humans are prone to make mistakes some-times, since he says about this *hadeeth* that in one narration 'Atiyyah says: "Aboo Sa'eed narrated to me," and he himself says about this: "Therefore through this we know that we are safe from 'Atiyyahs *tadlees*," as Ibn 'Alaan narrated from him, and some modern day authors follow him blindly in that. I say: This declaration that he heard it from him would only be of use if his *tadlees* were of the first type, but the *tadlees* of 'Atiyyah is of the second and worse type and will not be cured by this statement since he still said "Aboo Sa'eed narrated to me" which is exactly the evil type of *tadlees* which he is known for.[104]

So from what has preceded it will be clear that 'Atiyyah is weak due to his poor memory and evil *tadlees*, so this *hadeeth* of his is weak. As for the declaration of al-Haafidh that it is *hasan*, which has beguiled some people who have no knowledge, then it is founded upon inadvertence. So be aware and do not be amongst those who are unaware. In the *hadeeth* there are other weaknesses which I have spoken about in the aforementioned book, so there is no need to repeat them since whoever wishes can refer to that.

As for the understanding of some people today that the saying of al-Haafidh Ibn Hajr in *at-Taqreeb* amounts to declaration of the reliability of 'Atiyyah, then this is something which is not correct at all. I also asked Shaikh Ahmad ibn as-

---

104. From this it will become clear to the noble readers that those who still blindly follow al-Haafidh upon this saying after our explanation of the type of *tadlees* which 'Atiyyah is guilty of, then this person is biased and following his desires. This is the case with one who quoted this saying of al-Haafidh, using it as a reply to my declaration of the weakness of the *hadeeth*. I say that he is biased since I know that he is aware of the type of *tadlees* committed here and which is spoken of by me; this is because he is replying to these words of mine about this *hadeeth*. However he feigns ignorance of that fact and doesn't say a single word in reply to it. Rather he pretends that the *tadlees* was of the first kind which can be removed by a narration where it is clearly stated that a narrator heard it directly from his Shaikh. Will the readers excuse me if I say: Do such people not themselves deserve to be placed amongst those guilty of *tadlees* like 'Atiyyah?!

Siddeeq when I met him in the Zaahiriyyah Library in Damascus about this understanding and he too found it very strange. For when the mistakes of a narrator become many his reliability is destroyed, as opposed to one whose mistakes are few. The first of these is weak whereas the second is *hasan* in *hadeeth*. This is why al-Haafidh in *Sharhun-Nukhbah* says, that one whose mistakes are many is the partner of one whose memory is poor, and he declares the *ahaadeeth* of both of them to be rejected, so refer back to that along with the footnotes of Shaikh 'Alee al-Qaaree (pp.121&130).

These people have been deceived by what they report from al-Haafidh that he said in *Takhreejul-Adhkaar*: "The weakness of 'Atiyyah is due to his being a *Shee'ee*, and due to the fact that it is said that he committed *tadlees;* apart from this he is acceptable." So these people, due to their paucity of knowledge or their lack of knowledge, do not have the courage to explain their view that the scholars do indeed make mistakes. Rather they quote their words as if they are secure from any error or slip whatsoever, especially if their words agree with what they desire, such as is the case with this quote. Since it is clear here that these words run contrary to the saying of al-Haafidh in *at-Taqreeb* where he shows that 'Atiyyah is weak due to two reasons:

(i) Being a *Shee'ee*, which is not always a cause of weakness in the correct saying, and

(ii) *Tadlees* which is a weakness that can be removed as will follow. However he seemed to weaken this reason by saying: "It is said... " Whereas in *at-Taqreeb* he definitely stated that he is a *mudallis*, just as he declares him to be a *shee'ee*. Therefore al-Haafidh himself also says of him in *Tabaqaatul-Mudalliseen* (p.18): "A well-known *taabi'ee*, weak in memory and well-known for evil *tadlees*," and he mentions him in the fourth level about whom he says: "Those about whom there is agreement then none of their *hadeeth* are acceptable unless they state clearly that they heard it directly. This is due to their frequency in reporting by means of *tadlees* from weak and unknown narrators, such as Baqiyyah ibn al-Waleed."

He mentions this in his introduction. So both of these are clear statements from al-Haafidh himself which prove that he erred in the sentence in question when casting doubt upon the status of 'Atiyyah as a *mudallis*. This is one way in which there is contradiction between this saying and what is found in *at-Taqreeb*. Then a further way in which there is contradiction is that in the sentence in question he fails to describe him with what is another cause of his weakness, as has preceded from him in the quote from *Sharhun-Nukhbah*, and that is his saying in *at-Taqreeb*: "He makes many mistakes." All of this shows us that al-Haafidh, *rahimahullaah*, was not aided by his memory at the instance of his commenting upon this *hadeeth*. He therefore fell into this shortcoming which is witnessed to by his words in the other books which have more right to be depended upon. This is because in those books he quotes directly from the sources and abridges what they say, as opposed to what he does in *Takhreejul-Adhkaar*.

Due to the weakness of al-'Awfee a number of scholars have declared this *hadeeth* to be weak. Amongst them al-Haafidh al-Mundhiree in *at-Targheeb*,[105]and an-Nawawee, and Shaikhul-Islaam Ibn Taimiyyah in *al-Qaa'idatul-Jaaliyah* and likewise al-Boosayree who said in *Misbaahuz-Zujaajah* (2/52): "This chain of narration is comprised of a succession of weak narrators: 'Atiyyah and Fudayl ibn Marzooq and al-Fadl ibn al-Muwaffaq, all of them are weak." Also Siddeeq Hasan Khaan said in *Nuzulul-Abraar* (p.71), after quoting this *hadeeth* and the *hadeeth* of Bilaal which follows: "Their chains of narration are weak, as clearly stated by an-Nawawee in *al-Adhkaar*."

S e c o n d   H a d e e t h : The *hadeeth* of Bilaal which was indicated by Siddeeq Hasan Khaan is what is attributed to him that he said: "When Allaah's

---

105. He says (2/265): "Ibn Maajah reports it with a chain of narration which is criticised," and he declares it weak in another place (1/130-131), by introducing it with the words: "(*Ruwiya*) 'there is a report to the effect'..." by which he indicates that it is something which cannot be raised to the level of *hasan*, as he explains in his introduction.

Messenger (﷽) went out to the Prayer he used to say: 'In the name of Allaah, I believe in Allaah, I place my reliance upon Allaah, there is no action nor any strength except by (the will of) Allaah. O Allaah by the right of those who ask You, and by the right of this going out of mine, since I do not go out for evil, nor out of pride...' the *hadeeth*. It is reported by Ibn as-Sunnee in *al-'Uqaylee*, from Aboo Salamah ibn 'Abdur-Rahmaan, from Jaabir ibn 'Abdillaah, from him. This chain of narration is very weak and its problem is al-Waazi' [his name meaning 'restraint'] who did not have any restraint to prevent him from lying as I have explained in *Silsilatud-Da'eefah*. Therefore an-Nawawee says in *al-Adhkaar*: "The *hadeeth* is weak. One of its narrators, al-Waazi' ibn Naafi' al-'Uqaylee is weak by agreement, and he is severely weak (*munkar*)." Then al-Haafidh adds to this when commenting upon the *hadeeth*: "This is an extremely weak *hadeeth*. Ad-Daaraqutnee quotes it in this form in *al-Afraad* and said: "al-Waazi' is alone in reporting it and that they are agreed upon his weakness and that he is severely weak." Then the saying is actually more severe than that since Ibn Ma'een and an-Nasaa'ee said: "He is abandoned in *hadeeth*," and al-Haakim said: "He reports fabricated *hadeeth*.""[106]

So it is not permissible to use it as a proof, as was done by Shaikh al-Kawtharee, Shaikh al-Ghumaaree in *Misbaahuz-Zujaajah* (p.56) and other innovators. Then on top of the fact that these two *hadeeth* are weak, they also in no way contain any evidence at all for *tawassul* by means of a created being. Rather they both refer to one of the prescribed types of *tawassul* which have preced-

---

[106]. I said in *ad-Da'eefah* after speaking about this *hadeeth* of Bilaal, and the preceding *hadeeth*: "So in summary the *hadeeth* is weak by both narrations and one of them is more severely weak than the other." So some authors feigned ignorance of this sentence and then laid false accusation against me and said; "So it is clear that they are two separate *hadeeth* in their chains of narration, from the beginning to the end so how can it be correct for him to make these two into a single *hadeeth* and pass a single ruling upon them, this is a proof of the level of his confusion." I say: let the reader consider, are they truthful in what they claim, and then may they excuse me if I mention his (﷽) saying: *"From the speech of earlier Prophethood is: If you can feel no shame then do as you wish"*!

ed, and that is *tawassul* to Allaah, the Most High, by means of His attributes. This is because they both mention *tawassul* by means of those who make request to Allaah, and by the right of those who walk to the Prayer. What is the right of those who make request of Allaah? There is no doubt that it is that He should answer their supplication, and His answering the supplication of His worshippers is one of His attributes, He the Mighty and Majestic. Likewise the right of the Muslim who walks to the mosque is that Allaah should forgive him and enter him into Paradise, and the forgiveness of Allaah, the Most High, and His mercy, and His entering those who obey Him into His Paradise, all of these are attributes of His, He the Blessed and Most High. So from this it is known that the *hadeeth* which the innovators seek to use as a proof is in reality against them, and sound and correct understanding of it causes it to be a proof for us against them, and all praise and thanks are for Allaah for guiding to and granting that which is correct.

T h i r d   H a d e e t h : From Aboo Umaamah who said: "Allaah's Messenger (ﷺ) used to supplicate in the morning and the evening with this supplication: "O Allaah You have the most right of all who are mentioned, and the most right of all those who are worshipped ... I ask You by the light of Your Face which causes the heavens and the earth to shine brightly, and by every right which is Yours, and by the right of those who make request to You..." Al-Haithumee said in *Majma' uz-Zawaaid* (10/117): "At-Tabaraanee reported it and it contains Fadaalah ibn Jubayr, who is weak, and there is agreement upon his weakness." I say: Rather he is very weak: Ibn Hibbaan accuses him saying: "A Shaikh who claims that he heard from Aboo Umaamah. He reports from him things which are not from his *ahaadeeth*." He also said: "It is not permissible to use him as a proof in any circumstances, he reports *ahaadeeth* which have no basis at all." Ibn 'Adiyy said in *al-Kaamil* (25/13): "All of his *ahaadeeth* are things which are not preserved." I say: So the *hadeeth* is very weak and cannot be used as a proof at all, as was done by the author of *al-Misbaah* (p.56).

F o u r t h   H a d e e t h : From Anas ibn Maalik who said: "When Faatimah bint Asad ibn Haashim, the mother of 'Alee, *radiyallaahu 'anhumaa*, died, he called Usaamah ibn Zayd, Aboo Ayyoob al-Ansaaree, 'Umar ibn al-Khattaab, and a young black boy to dig the grave... then when they had finished Allaah's Messenger (ﷺ) entered and lay her down there and said: "It is Allaah who gives life and gives death, and He is the Ever-Living who never dies, forgive my mother Faatimah bint Asad, and grant her her proof, and grant her a spacious place by the right of Your Prophet, and the Prophets who came before me, for indeed You are the Most-Merciful of those who show mercy..." Al-Haithumee said in *Majma' uz-Zawaa'id* (9/257): "At-Tabaraanee reports it in *al-Kabeer* and *al-Awsat* and it contains Rawh ibn as-Salaah who is declared reliable by Ibn Hibbaan and al-Haakim, but is somewhat weak. Then the rest of its narrators are those of the *Saheeh*." I say: By way of at-Tabaraanee it is reported by Aboo Nu'aym in *Hilyatul-Awliyaa* (3/121) and their chain of narration is weak since Rawh ibn as-Salaah who is one of its narrators is alone in narrating it, as Aboo Nu'aym himself said. Then Rawh is declared to be weak by Ibn 'Adiyy, and Ibn Yoonus said: "Weak and reprehensible things are reported from him." Ad-Daaraqutnee said: "He is *da'eef* (weak) in *hadeeth*." Ibn Maakoolaa said: "They declare him weak." Ibn 'Adiyy said after quoting two of his *hadeeth*: "He reports many *ahaadeeth* and some of them are reprehensible." So they agree upon his weakness, so his *hadeeth* is weak (*munkar*) since he is alone in reporting it. There are some people who try to strengthen this *hadeeth* based upon the declaration of Ibn Hibbaan and al-Haakim that Rawh is reliable. However this will not benefit them due to what is known with regard to their leniency in declaration of reliability. So this saying of theirs when opposed by sayings of other scholars does not carry any weight even if the declaration of weakness by the other scholars is not explained, so how about when the reason for weakness is made clear as is the case here? I have also fully explained the weakness of this *hadeeth* in *ad-Da'eefah* (no.23) and so I will not repeat that here. The antagonists whom we have indicated quote that which can only cause laughter, saying: "Shaikh Naasir judged it to be weak, so we ask that he tell us who from the scholars of *hadeeth* has declared this *hadeeth* weak." We quoted those who declare its narrator Rawh ibn as-Salaah to be weak, and he is alone in narrating it. This automatically means weakness of the *hadeeth* unless someone is found to report it along with him, and Aboo Nu'aym had denied that there is anyone supporting his narration, unless another narration of it is found, and that is not the case! Then they say: "Even if we accept that it is weak, then it is only slightly weak which would not prevent action upon it, since it is a case of acting on a *hadeeth* whose weakness is not severe in that which relates to mere encouragements and warnings, which is allowed by the scholars of *hadeeth* and *fiqh*." I say: There is no encouragement in this *hadeeth*, nor does it explain some excellence for an action which is already established as being prescribed in the *Sharee'ah*. Rather it is speaking about something which may be permissible or may not be permissible, therefore it is being used to establish a *Sharee'ah* ruling, if it were authentic. Furthermore these people are quoting it as a proof for this form of *tawassul* about which there is a disagreement. So when you accept its weakness, then it is not permissible to use it as a proof. I do not think any intelligent person would agree that it pertains to mere encouragements and warnings. Rather this is the way of those who flee away from submission to the truth, they say things which no intelligent person would say.

F i f t h   H a d e e t h : From Umayyah ibn 'Abdillaah ibn Khaalid ibn Usayd, who said: "Allaah's Messenger (ﷺ) used to seek victory by means of the weak Muhaajirs."

So the antagonists think that the *hadeeth* shows that the Prophet (ﷺ) used to ask Allaah, the Most High, to grant him victory due to the weak and poor from the Muhaajirs, and this, as they claim, was the same as this form of *tawassul* about which there is disagreement. So the reply to this is from two angles:

(i) The *hadeeth* is weak. It is reported by at-Tabaraanee in *al-Kabeer* (1/81/2): Muhammad ibn Ishaaq ibn Raahooyah narrated to us: my father narrated to me: 'Eesaa ibn Yoonus narrated to us: my father narrated to me: from his father[107]: from Umayyah with it." Also: "'Abdullaah ibn Muhammad ibn 'Abdil 'Azeez al-Baghawee narrated to us: 'Ubaydullaah ibn 'Umar al-Qawaareeree narrated to us: Yahyaa ibn Sa'eed narrated to us: from Sufyaan: from Aboo Ishaaq: from Umayyah ibn Khaalid from the Prophet (ﷺ) with the wording: "... he used to fight and seek victory by means of the weak Muslims." I say: Its narration rests solely upon Umayyah, and it is not established that he was a Companion, so the *hadeeth* is *mursal*[108]and weak. Ibn 'Abdur-Barr said in *al-Istee'aab* (1/38): "It is not correct with me that he was a Companion, and the *hadeeth* is *mursal*." Also al-Haafidh says in *al-Isaabah* (1/133): "He was not a Companion and did not hear anything from him (ﷺ) to narrate." I say: It also has another weakness which is that Aboo Ishaaq deteriorated in later life and also his being a *mudallis* and reporting by means of *'an'anah*[109]. However Sufyaan heard narrations from him before he deteriorated, so that only leaves the other weakness which is his reporting by means of *''an'anah'*. So it is established that the *hadeeth* is weak and cannot be used to establish proof. That is the first answer.

(ii) Even if the *hadeeth* were authentic then it would indicate nothing except what is indicated by the *hadeeth* of 'Umar and the *hadeeth* of the blind man, which is *tawassul* by means of the supplication of the pious. Al-Manaawee said in *Faydul-Qadeer*: "'He used to request aid' means: he used to seek aid in the fighting, as occurs in the Saying of Allaah, the Most High,

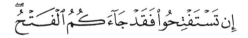

"(O disbelievers) if you ask for a judgement, now has the judgement come unto you."[110]

---

107. Who was Aboo Ishaaq as-Sabee'ee.

108. i.e. their is a missing link between the final narrator and the Prophet (ﷺ).

109. Saying 'from so and so' and not making clear whether he heard it directly from him or not.

110. Soorah Al-Anfaal (8): 19.

"It was mentioned by az-Zamakhsharee, 'he sought victory by means of the poor Muslims,' means: by means of the supplication of the poor who had no wealth."

This explanation also occurs in his (ﷺ) *hadeeth*, which is reported by an-Nasaa'ee (2/15) with the wording: *Indeed Allaah gives victory to this Ummah due to its weak ones, through their supplication, their Prayers and their purity of intention.* Its chain of narration is authentic, and the basis of it occurs in *Saheehul-Bukhaaree* [transl. 4/94/no.145] so the *hadeeth* shows that seeking the victory was done by means of the supplication of the pious, not by means of their person or status.

This is further confirmed by the fact that the *hadeeth* with the previous wording reported by Qays ibn ar-Rabee' was: "He used to seek aid in the fighting and victory..." So we know that his seeking victory by means of the pious was by means of their supplications, Prayers and purity of intention and likewise with regard to his seeking aid in the fighting. So this *hadeeth,* if authentic, is a further proof for the prescribed form of *tawassul*, and a proof against the innovated type of *tawassul*, and all praise and thanks are for Allaah.

S i x t h   H a d e e t h : From 'Umar ibn al-Khattaab from the Prophet (ﷺ): "When Aadam fell into the sin he said: 'O my Lord, I ask You by the right of Muhammad to forgive me.' He said: 'O Aadam, and how do you know of Muhammad when I have not yet created him?' He said: "O my Lord when You created me with Your Hand, and breathed life into me, I raised up my head and saw written upon the pillars of the Throne: 'None has the right to be worshipped except Allaah, Muhammad is the Messenger of Allaah.' So I knew that You would not add after your name that of anyone except the most beloved of the creation to You." So He said: 'I have forgiven you, and if it were not for Muhammad I would not have created you.'" It is reported by al-Haakim in *al-Mustadrak* (2/615) by way of Abul-Haarith 'Abdullaah ibn Muslim al-Fihree: Ismaa'eel ibn Maslamah narrated to us: 'Abdur-Rahmaan ibn Zayd ibn Aslam related to us: from his father: from his grandfather: from 'Umar, and he said: "*Saheeh* of *isnaad* and it is the first *hadeeth* of 'Abdur-Rahmaan ibn Zayd ibn Aslam which I have mentioned in this book." Adh-Dhahabee criticises him, saying: "I say: Rather it is fabricated (*mawdoo'*) and 'Abdur-Rahmaan is severely weak (*waahin*), and as for 'Abdullaah ibn Aslam al-Fihree, then I do not know who he is." I say: From the self-contradiction of al-Haakim in *al-Mustadrak* is that he reports another *hadeeth* of this same 'Abdur-Rahmaan (3/332) and does not declare it authentic, but rather said: "The two Shaikhs do not accept 'Abdur-Rahmaan ibn Zayd as a proof!"

With regard to al-Fihree, adh-Dhahabee mentions him in *al-Meezaan* and quotes this *hadeeth* of his and then says: "A baseless and futile narration." The same is said by al-Haafidh Ibn Haajr in *al-Lisaan* (3/360) and he adds to his saying about al-Fihree: "And I do not think it to be unlikely that he is one and the same person as the one just quoted since he is of the same level and time." I say: The narrator whom he spoke of before him was 'Abdullaah ibn Muslim ibn Rushayd, about whom al-Haafidh said: "Ibn Hibbaan mentions him, he is accused of fabricating *ahaadeeth*. He fabricates narrations which he attributes to Layth, Maalik and Ibn Lahee'ah. It is not permissible to write down his *ahaadeeth*. He is the one who narrated a manuscript of *hadeeth* from Ibn Lahee'ah, and it seems to be something deliberately invented."

The *hadeeth* is also reported by at-Tabaraanee in *al-Mu'jamus-Sagheer* (p.207): "Muhammad ibn Daawood ibn Aslam as-Sadafee al-Misree narrated to us: Ahmad ibn Sa'eed al-Madanee al-Fihree narrated to us: 'Abdullaah ibn Ismaa'eel al-Madanee narrated to us: from 'Abdur-Rahmaan ibn Zayd ibn Aslam with it." This chain of narration is murky since all the narrators before 'Abdur-Rahmaan are unknown and this is also indicated by al-Haafidh al-Haithamee in *Mujama' uz-Zawaa'id* (8/253) where he says: "It is reported by at-Tabaraanee in *al-Awsat* and *as-Sagheer* and contains narrators whom I do not know." I say: This is a deficient declaration of weakness since it gives the impression to those who have no knowledge that it does not have any narrators who are known for their weakness. This is not the case since its narrations rest upon 'Abdur-Rahmaan ibn Zayd ibn Aslam, and al-Baihaqee said: "He alone reports it," and he is accused of fabrication, of which he is accused by al-Haakim himself. The scholars therefore criticise him for his declaration of the authenticity of this *hadeeth* and they declare that to be an error and a contradiction. So 'the inheritor of the knowledge of the Companions, the *taabi'een* and the imaams who are followed, Shaikhul-Islaam Ibn Taimiyyah'[111], *rahimahullaah*, said in *al-Qaa'idatul-Jaliyyah* (p.89): "Al-Haakim's reporting this *hadeeth* is something for which, he is to be criticised since he himself said in his book: *al-Madkhal ilaa Ma'rifatis-Saheeh minas-Saqeem*: "'Abdur-Rahmaan ibn Zayd ibn Aslam reported fabricated *ahaadeeth* from his father, and it will not be hidden from the experts in this field who examine them that he is to blame for them.[112] I say: 'Abdur-Rahmaan ibn Zayd ibn Aslam is weak by agreement of the scholars, and he made many mistakes.[113] He was declared weak by Ahmad ibn Hanbal, Aboo Zur'ah, an-Nasaaee, ad-Daaraqutnee and others. Ibn Hibbaan said: 'He used to mix up the narrations and not be aware, to the point that he did it frequently. He would connect things which were *mursal* and quote sayings as being those of the Prophet (ﷺ) which were *mawqoof* (stopped at the level of the Companion), so he deserved to be abandoned. As for the authentication which al-Haakim gave to this *hadeeth* and its like, then this is something for which the scholars of *hadeeth* criticised him, and they declared that al-Haakim even authenticates narrations which are fabrications and lies, known to those having knowledge of *hadeeth*. Therefore the scholars of *hadeeth* do not rely upon the authentication of al-Haakim on its own.'"

---

111. As he was described by the scholar, Shaikh Muhibbuddeen al-Khateeb in his introduction to the book: *al-Qaa'idatul-Jaliyyah*.

112. These words are also reported from al-Haakim and Ibn Hibbaan by al-Haafidh Ibn 'Abdul-Haadee in *as-Saarimul-Munkee* (p.29) and al-Haafidh Ibn Hajr in *at-Tahdheeb*.

113. This is a clear statement from Shaikhul-Islaam that the phrase 'he makes many mistakes' is a wording of criticism, not any sort of declaration of reliability and as can be seen there is no difference between it and between the saying: 'he makes many errors' which is the phrase used by al-Haafidh to describe 'Atiyyah al-'Awfee, as has preceded.

Al-Haakim himself mentions 'Abdur-Rahmaan ibn Zayd ibn Aslam in his book of weak narrators *ad-Du'afaa*, as it is named by the scholar Ibn 'Abdul-Haadee and he says at the end of it: "Those narrators whom I have mentioned, are those who are declared weak with true and clear reason, since declaration of weakness is only established due to a clear proof, and so these are people whose weakness I can clearly explain to anyone who asks about that, since I do not allow declaration of weakness based on blindly following the saying of another. So what I prefer for the student of this knowledge is that he does not write a single *hadeeth* from those people whom I have named. The one who narrates their *hadeeth* falls under his (ﷺ) saying: *Whoever narrates a hadeeth knowing it to be a lie, then he is one of the liars.*"[114]

Whoever carefully considers this saying of al-Haakim and that which came before it will clearly see that this *hadeeth* of 'Abdur-Rahmaan ibn Zayd is a fabrication even in the view of al-Haakim himself, and that whoever narrates it after knowing his status is himself one of the liars. The sayings of the preservers of *hadeeth*: Ibn Taimiyyah, adh-Dhahabee and Ibn Hajr al-'Asqalaanee are in agreement that this *hadeeth* is baseless. They are agreed with in that conclusion by other verifying scholars such as al-Haafidh Ibn 'Abdul-Haadee as will follow. So it is not permissible for one who believes in Allaah and the Last Day to declare the *hadeeth* authentic after the agreement of these scholars that it is weak; and it is not permissible to declare it authentic merely due to blind acceptance of one of the two sayings of al-Haakim, especially when in the other saying he preferred that the student of knowledge should not write down this *hadeeth* of 'Abdur-Rahmaan and that by doing so he would be one of the liars, as has preceded.

---

114. Reported by Muslim in the introduction to his *Saheeh* and Ibn Hibbaan in his *Saheeh* (1/27) from the *hadeeth* of Samurah ibn Jundub, and Muslim from the *hadeeth* of al-Mugheerah ibn Shu'bah, and he said: "It is a well-known *hadeeth*."

NOTE: When you know this, then you will see that the saying of some Shaikhs: "The ruling of Shaikh Naasir upon this *hadeeth* that it is a lie and a fabrication is itself futile because it is based on the saying of adh-Dhahabee that is fabricated," This is it itself a futile saying since adh-Dhahabee was agreed to in that by the prominent preservers of *hadeeth* whom we have mentioned. Then they say: "The basis for adh-Dhahabee's saying was just that there is a man whom it is said - is accused in the *isnaad* of al-Haakim" I say: This is also futile since the man in question was 'Abdullaah ibn Muslim al-Fihree who adh-Dhahabee said was unknown to him, and he did not accuse him, as has preceded. I do not think this fact is hidden from them, but they feign ignorance of it for their own ends, and that is so that they are then able to follow that by saying: "However the *hadeeth* has another chain of narration reported by at-Tabaraanee which does not contain this person who is accused, and the most that can be said against it is that it contains narrator/s who is/are not well-known." I say: Rather it contains three narrators who are not known, and if they do not know that then why do they turn away from blindly following what al-Haythumee said in his saying: "It contains those whom I do not know," as has preceded, since they are a people who blindly follow to the point of destruction, but here they prefer to say: "It contains narrator/s who is/are not well-known"?! The reason for this is that the saying of al-Haithumee is a clear statement that it is actually a number of people who are unknown, whereas their wording does not show that. Rather their wording could cover a single unknown narrator or more, so in reality it is an attempt to hide the truth from the readers, and we seek Allaah's refuge from disgrace. Then in addition they say after what has preceded: "And it also contains 'Abdur-Rahmaan ibn Zayd and he in the saying preferred by al-Haafidh Ibn Hajr - is that he is one of those who are said to be weak, and that is the least severe of the levels of weakness."

I say: However the correct saying with other than al-Haafidh is that he is more severely weak than that. Aboo Nu'aym said about him: "He reports fabricated *ahaadeeth* from his father." Al-Haakim himself said the same thing as has preceded, and both he and Aboo Nu'aym are amongst those known for leniency in declaring narrators reliable. So when they so declare this narrator weak, then it is because it has become clear to them that 'Abdur-Rahmaan is truly weak. Therefore the scholars are agreed upon his being weak, as was stated by Shaikhul-Islaam Ibn Taimiyyah, *rahimahullaah*. Indeed he is declared to be very weak by 'Alee ibn al-Madeenee, Ibn Sa'd and others, and at-Tahaawee said: "His *hadeeth*, are to the scholars of *hadeeth*, at the extreme of weakness." So from early to late times he was known for severe weakness, so what has caused the antagonists to turn away from these sayings which are united in declaring that 'Abdur-Rahmaan is very weak, if not a liar, and instead to cling to the saying of al-Haafidh about him that he is "weak"?! I say this along with the possibility that it could have been a slip of the pen of al-Haafidh or one of the transmitters, missing out the word 'very' along with 'weak'.

But anyway their blind-following of al-Haafidh upon this word will be of no benefit to them after he himself has judged the *hadeeth* to be a "baseless and futile narration" as has been quoted from *al-Lisaan*! So this is one of the many proofs that these people are followers of desires and not seekers after the truth. If they were then they would have accepted this particular saying of al-Haafidh which agrees with that of adh-Dhahabee and others from the verifying scholars. They would not turn to his other saying that 'Abdur-Rahmaan was merely 'weak', in order to use this in opposition to the saying of adh-Dhahabee, and to give a false impression of this *hadeeth* to the people, making it appear as if it is a *hadeeth* about which the scholars differ. This will then make it easy for them to invent a new view about the *hadeeth* which appears to conform with the saying of one of the scholars about one of its narrators! See what they finally say after what has preceded from them: "So when that is the case with someone in the view of the scholars of *hadeeth*, then it is not a fabrication, nor is it something very weak. Rather it is of the level of those narrations which can be acted upon with regard to virtuous actions"! This is invalid from two angles: Firstly: that it is based upon the fact that 'Abdur-Rahmaan is merely 'weak', and that is not the case. Rather he is 'very weak' (*da'eef jiddan*) as has preceded, and a clear statement of this from one of the critical preservers of *hadeeth* will follow. Secondly: it contradicts the ruling of al-Haafidh himself upon it, indeed the ruling of other scholars also, that the *hadeeth* is baseless, as has preceded. So how is it permissible for them to contradict them, especially when one of them stated in *at-Ta'qeebul-Hatheeth* (p.21), that he "does not possess the ability to declare things authentic or weak!" So perhaps he said that out of modesty! Since here you see that he has given himself a station that allows him to come to his own independent conclusion even if it means that he contradicts these critical scholars! What we say about him is supported by the fact that he further adds to what had preceded: "So with regard to this *hadeeth* we share the view of those who do not hold that [i.e. that it is fabricated], such as al-Haakim and al-Haafidh as-Subkee. So we do not wish to rebut al-Haafidh adh-Dhahabee, however our view is that the position of these two scholars is closer to the truth."

The fact that this saying contains deception and hides the true reality can be seen clearly since al-Haakim declares the *hadeeth* authentic in *al-Mustadrak*, as has preceded, and then as-Subkee merely blindly accepted that from him as explained by al-Haafidh Ibn 'Abdul-Haadee, who says in his reply to as-Subkee entitled *as-Saarimul-Munkee* (p.32): "I am amazed at how he blindly follows al-Haakim in declaring the *hadeeth* authentic since it is a *hadeeth* which is neither authentic nor established. Indeed it is a *hadeeth* whose chain of narration is very weak, and some of the scholars have adjudged it to be fabricated. Its chain of narration from al-Haakim to 'Abdur-Rahmaan ibn Zayd is not even authentic, rather it was falsely attached to 'Abdur-Rahmaan as we will explain. Even if it were authentic up to 'Abdur-Rahmaan it would still be weak and not a proof since 'Abdur-Ramaan is in its chain, and al-Haakim had made a very great contradiction, as he is known to have done in various places. This is because he said in his book *ad-Du'aafaa*, after mentioning 'Abdur-Rahmaan amongst the weak narrators..." and he then mentions what has preceded (see p.101) and then says: "So see the great error and serious contradiction that al-Haakim has fallen into here. Then this miserable adversary took up this mistake and contradiction of al-Haakim, blindly following him upon it and relied upon it, saying: 'And in declaring it authentic we have relied upon al-Haakim.' Whereas a short while before he claimed that it was something whose authenticity had become clear to him. So look, may Allaah have mercy upon you, at this clear wretchedness and serious error! How this person came upon a *hadeeth* which is not authentic, and not established, rather it is a fabricated *hadeeth*, and he declared it authentic and relied upon in, blindly following al-Haakim in that even after his error and contradiction was clear. Even when this adversary knew of the weakness of its narrator and what is against him and was well aware of what has been said about him." I say: This was the case with as-Subkee, *rahimahullaah*, with regard to this *hadeeth*, and he blindly followed al-Haakim, in declaring it authentic. Along with the fact that this error is an error in itself, it is also contrary to the view which these people hold, i.e. that it is weak, not authentic and not fabricated, so these people and those who blindly-follow and support them have contradicted al-Haakim and as-Subkee, just as they have contradicted the other great scholars whom we have mentioned who declare the *hadeeth* to be fabricated or baseless. So they are not just rebutting adh-Dhahabee only, but rather all those who have agreed or even differed with him also! So let the intelligent person see what following of desires does to a person! They want to free themselves of the charge of rebutting adh-Dhahabee, and can only do so by saying that which is worse, which is to rebut all the scholars whom we have mentioned!

A further error of theirs which is clear to the people of knowledge is something else that they say during their previous words which is that they mention the chain of narration of at-Tabaraanee which we have already spoken about and they say: "So adh-Dhahabee did not come across this chain of narration, since if he had he would not have said that." This is a futile saying since adh-Dhahabee judged the *hadeeth* to be baseless and futile by way of al-Haakim, and his narration contains 'Abdur-Rahmaan ibn Zayd and another man whom he did not know, as has preceded. The narration of at-Tabaraanee has in addition to the same 'Abdur-Rahmaan three other unknown narrators, so how can it be correct to then say that if adh-Dhahabee had seen it he would not have said?! By Allaah this is a clear case of error and arrogance, or ignorance of the true state of their own ignorance! So we ask for Allaah's mercy and guidance! From what has preceded it will become clear to the noble readers that the *hadeeth* has two weaknesses:

(i) 'Abdur-Rahmaan ibn Zayd ibn Aslam who is very weak.
(ii) Unknown narrators in the chain of narration up to 'Abdur-Rahmaan.

In my view the *hadeeth* has a further weakness which is self-contradiction (*idti-raab*) by 'Abdur-Rahmaan or one beyond him in the chain. This is because sometimes he reported it as the saying of the Prophet (ﷺ), as has preceded, and sometimes he reported it as the saying of 'Umar alone, not from the Prophet (ﷺ), as it is reported by Aboo Bakr al-Aajurree in his book *ash-Sharee'ah* (p.427), by way of 'Abdullaah ibn Ismaa'eel ibn Abee Maryam, from: 'Abdur-Rahmaan ibn Zayd with it. As for this narrator 'Abdullaah then I do not know him. So this is not authentic from 'Umar, neither as the saying of the Prophet (ﷺ), nor as the saying of 'Umar. Al-Aajurree reports it by another chain from 'Abdur-Rahmaan ibn Abiz-Zinaad, from his father; that he said: "From the words because of which Allaah forgave Aadam were his saying: 'O Allaah I ask You by the right of Muhammad upon You...' in similar but abridged form. This along with the fact that the final link/s in its chain is/are missing, and that it is not quoted as the saying of the Prophet (ﷺ), then in addition to this its chain of narration up to Ibn Abiz-Zinaad is also weak, containing 'Uthmaan ibn Khaalid the father of Marwaan al-'Uthmaanee. an-Nasaae'e said of him: "He is not at all reliable." Therefore it is not unlikely that this *hadeeth* is from those things taken from the people of the Book which are introduced amongst the Muslims by people of the Book who accepted *Islaam*, or from those who did not, or taken from their Books which are not dependable due to the changes and distortions which they suffered, as explained by Shaikhul-Islaam in his books. One of those weak narrators could have attributed that to the Prophet (ﷺ) either mistakenly or deliberately.

HOW THIS *HADEETH* CONTRADICTS THE *QUR'AAN*

The view held by the scholars that this *hadeeth* is a baseless fabrication is further supported by the fact that it contradicts the Noble Qur'aan in two places. Firstly: That it declares that Allaah, the Most High, forgave Aadam because of his *tawassul* by means of the Prophet (ﷺ), whereas Allaah, the Mighty and Majestic says:

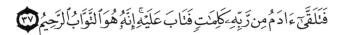

"Then Aadam received from his Lord Words. And his Lord pardoned him (accepted his repentance). Verily, He is the One Who forgives (accepts repentance), the Most Merciful."[115]

The explanation of what these words were has been explained by the great explainer of the Qur'aan Ibn 'Abbaas, *radiyallaahu 'anhumaa*, and this explanation is contrary to this *hadeeth*. So al-Haakim reports (3/545) from him, concerning the meaning of the *Aayah*: "He said: 'O my Lord did You not create me with Your Hand?' He said: "Yes indeed." He said: "Did You not breathe life into me?" He said: "Yes indeed." He said: "O my Lord did You not make me an inhabitant of Your Paradise?" He said: "Yes indeed." He said: "Does not Your mercy take precedence over Your anger?" He said: "Yes indeed." He said: "Then if I repent and amend will You return me to Paradise?" He said: "Yes indeed." He [Ibn 'Abbaas] said: "So that is His saying: فَتَلَقَّىٰٓ ءَادَمُ مِن رَّبِّهِۦ كَلِمَٰتٍ ." al-Haakim said: "Its chain of narration is *saheeh*" and adh-Dhahabee agreed with him, and it is as they say.

This saying of Ibn 'Abbaas carries the ruling of being the saying of the Prophet (ﷺ) due to two reasons:

---

115. Soorah Al-Baqarah (2): 37.

(i) It is speaking about a matter from the Hidden and Unseen, which cannot be spoken about with mere opinion, and

(ii) That it is reported in explanation of the *Aayah* and whatever is such as that has that ruling as is affirmed in its place, particularly when it is from the words of the imaam of the scholars of *tafseer*, 'Abdullaah ibn 'Abbaas, *radiyallaahu 'anhumaa*, for whom the Prophet (ﷺ) supplicated: *O Allaah grant him understanding in the religion, and teach him correct explanation.*[116]

It is also said in explanation of these *words* that they are what occurs in another *Aayah*:

"They said (Aadam and Eve): 'Our Lord! We have wronged ourselves. If You forgive us not, and bestow not upon us Your Mercy, we shall certainly be of the losers.'"[117]

This is what as-Sayyid Rasheed Ridaa states to be correct in his *Tafseer* (1/279), however Ibn Katheer indicates the weakness of that (1/81). To me there is no contradiction between the two sayings, rather one is a completion of the other. So the *hadeeth* of Ibn 'Abbaas does not mention the words of repentance which Aadam, *'alaihis-salaam*, learned from his Lord, whereas this second saying mentions what they are. So there is no contradiction, and all praise and thanks are for Allaah, whereas the contradiction of the *hadeeth* in question is confirmed, and it is thus baseless.

---

116. *Musnad Ahmad* (1/266).

117. Al-'Araaf (7): 23

The second place is what occurs at the end of it: "If it were not for Muhammad I would not have created You." This is a very serious matter relating to belief and creed ('aqeedah), which is to be established by a *mutawaatir* text which they all agree to, or by any authentic text, as held by others.[118] If this were something authentic it would be reported in the Book or the authentic *Sunnah*. So holding this to be something authentic when there is no text sufficient to establish proof runs contrary to the Saying of Allaah, the Blessed and the Most High,:

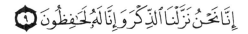

"Verily it is We Who have sent down the *Dhikr* and surely, We will guard it (from corruption)."[119]

The '*dhikr*' here comprises the whole *Sharee'ah*, both what is found in the Qur'aan and the *Sunnah*, as is affirmed by Ibn Hazm in *al-Ihkaam*. Allaah, the Blessed and the Most High, says:

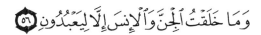

"And I (Allaah) created not the Jinns and humans except they should worship Me (alone)."[120]

So anyone who wishes to disagree with this stated purpose, or to add something to it, then that will not be accepted from him unless he produces an authentic text for it from the infallible Messenger(ﷺ). This applies to the con-

---

118. Translator's note: Refer to the book *The Hadeeth is Proof itself in Belief and Laws* by Shaikh al-Albaanee (Dar of Islamic Heritage, USA).

119. Soorah Al-Hijr (15): 9

120. Soorah Adh-Dhaariyaat (51): 56

tradiction of this baseless *hadeeth* and what is also often heard upon the tongues of the people: "Were it not for you, were it not for you, I would not have created the stars." So this is also a fabricated (*mawdoo'*) narration as pointed out by as-San'aanee and agreed to by ash-Shawkaanee in *al-Fawaaidul-Majmoo'ah fil-Ahaadeethil-Mawdoo'ah* (p.116). It is also curious how the false claimant to Prophethood Mirza Ghulaam Ahmad al-Qaadiyaanee stole this fabricated *hadeeth*, and then claimed that it was something which Allaah addressed him with, saying: "Were it not for you I would not have created the stars"!! This is something which is admitted by his followers the Qaadiyaanis here in Damascus and other places, since it is recorded in the book of their false claimant to Prophethood: *Haqeeqatul-Wahy* (p.99).

Even if it were possible to accept the claims that the *hadeeth* in question is only weak, as is claimed by some of them in contradiction to the scholars and pre-servers of *hadeeth* whom we have mentioned, then still it would not be per-missible to use it as a proof for the correctness of the form of *tawassul* about which there is disagreement. This is because it is according to their saying a prescribed form of worship, and the least level of any form of worship is that it is something recommended (*mustahabb*), and recommendation is one of the five levels of *Sharee'ah* rulings which cannot be established except through an authentic text sufficient to establish proof. So if someone holds that the *hadeeth* is weak then there can be no proof on it for him at all. This is very clear, if Allaah wills.

S e v e n t h   H a d e e t h : "Make *tawassul* by means of my status, for my status with Allaah is very great." Some of them report it with the wording: "When you ask Allaah, then ask Him by my status, for my status with Allaah is very great."

This is totally baseless; it is not reported in any of the books of *hadeeth* at all. Rather it is quoted by some people who are ignorant of the *Sunnah*, as point-ed out by Shaikhul-Islaam Ibn Taimiyyah, *rahimahullaah*, in *al-Qaa'idatul-*

117

Jaliyyah (p.132-150) where he says: "Even though his (ﷺ) status with Allaah is greater than the status of all the Prophets and the Messengers, however the status of the creation with the Creator is not like the status of created beings with other created beings. Indeed no one can intercede with Him except after His permission, whereas created beings may intercede with other created beings even without permission. So the created being is with regard to attainment of what is desired a partner of the other person involved, whereas Allaah, the Most High, has no partners, as He, the One free of any blemish or defect, says:

$$قُلِ ٱدْعُوا۟ ٱلَّذِينَ زَعَمْتُم مِّن دُونِ ٱللَّهِ لَا يَمْلِكُونَ مِثْقَالَ ذَرَّةٍ فِى ٱلسَّمَٰوَٰتِ وَلَا فِى ٱلْأَرْضِ وَمَا لَهُمْ فِيهِمَا مِن شِرْكٍ وَمَا لَهُۥ مِنْهُم مِّن ظَهِيرٍ ۝ وَلَا تَنفَعُ ٱلشَّفَٰعَةُ عِندَهُۥٓ إِلَّا لِمَنْ أَذِنَ لَهُۥ حَتَّىٰٓ إِذَا فُزِّعَ عَن قُلُوبِهِمْ قَالُوا۟ مَاذَا قَالَ رَبُّكُمْ قَالُوا۟ ٱلْحَقَّ وَهُوَ ٱلْعَلِىُّ ٱلْكَبِيرُ$$

"Say: (O Muhammad) 'Call upon those whom you assert (to be gods) besides Allaah, they possess not even the weight of an atom, - either in the heavens or on the earth, nor have they any share in either, nor is there for Him any supporter from among them. Intercession with Him profits not, except for him who He permits. Until when fear is banished from their (angels') hearts, they (the angels) say:'What is it that your Lord has said?' They say: 'The truth. And He is the Most High, the Most Great.'"[121]

---

121. Soorah Saba (34): 22-23

So the fact that his (ﷺ) status is very great with his Lord does not mean that we should make *tawassul* by it to Allaah, the Most High, since there is no order to do that established from him (ﷺ). This is clarified by the fact that *rukoo'* (bowing) and *sujood* (prostrating) are signs of veneration well-known to the people, and they used to - and some of them still do - stand up, bow and prostrate to their kings, presidents and those whom they respect. Then, as is agreed upon by the Muslims, Muhammad (ﷺ) is the greatest of all people and the highest of station. But is it permissible to stand up, bow or prostrate for him in his lifetime or after his death? The answer is that if anyone wishes to declare that lawful then he must prove that it is established in the *Sharee'ah*. But on examination we find that *sujood* and *rukoo'* are not permissible except to Allaah, the One free of all imperfections and the Most High, and the Prophet (ﷺ) forbade that anyone should bow or prostrate to anyone. Likewise we find in the *Sunnah* that the Prophet (ﷺ) hated that people should stand up for others, which shows that it is not prescribed. Do you think that anyone can claim that when we forbid anyone to prostrate to the Messenger (ﷺ) we are denying his (ﷺ) status and honour? No not at all. So likewise can anyone affirm that we should bow and prostrate to the Messenger (ﷺ) because of the fact that the Messenger (ﷺ) has great status? The answer is again, no, certainly not.

This clearly enables us to see, if Allaah wills, that the fact that it is established that the Prophet (ﷺ) has great status does not mean that we should honour him by making *tawassul* by means of his status, as long as that is not established in the *Sharee'ah*.

From his (ﷺ) great status is that it is made obligatory upon us that we follow him and obey him just as we have to obey his Lord. So it is established from him (ﷺ) that he said: *I have not left anything which brings you closer to Allaah except that I have ordered you with it.*[122]

---

122. Reported by ash-Shaafi'ee, at-Tabaraanee and others.

119

Since he did not order us with this type of *tawassul*, not even with an order of recommendation, then it is not worship. So we must follow him in that and leave our emotions to one side, and we should not become so lax as to start entering things into the religion which are not from it due to claims that we are displaying love of the Prophet (ﷺ). Rather true and sincere love is shown by truly following him (ﷺ), not by innovating new things, as Allaah, the Mighty and Majestic, says:

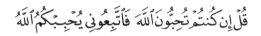

"Say (O Muhammad to mankind): 'If you (really) love Allaah then follow me, Allaah will love you.'"[123]

Also, as a poet said:
"You disobey God, yet you claim love of him:
This is indeed an astonishing state of affairs.
For if your love were sincere you would obey him:
Since a person is obedient to one whom he truly loves."

TWO WEAK REPORTS

The First Report: A narration about their seeking rain by means of the Messenger (ﷺ) after his death.

After having quoted the weak and inauthentic *ahaadeeth* and examining them we should now quote a report (*athar*) which is often quoted by those who permit this innovated form of *tawassul* in order to explain whether it is authentic or weak, and whether it is pertinent to the discussion or not?

Al-Haafidh says in *al-Fath* (2/397):
"Ibn Abee Shaybah reports with an authentic chain of narration, from the nar-

---

123. Soorah Aali-'Imraan (3): 31

ration of Aboo Saalih as-Samaan from Maalik ad-Daar, who was the treasurer for 'Umar, he said: "The people suffered from drought in the time of 'Umar, so a man came to the grave of the Prophet (ﷺ) and said: "O Messenger of Allaah! Pray for rain for your *Ummah*, because they are being destroyed." So someone came to the man in his dream and said: 'Go to 'Umar...' the *hadeeth*." Then Sayf reports in *al-Futooh* that the one who saw the dream was Bilaal ibn al-Haarith al-Muzaanee, one of the Companions."

The reply to this is from a number of angles:

1 . We do not accept that this story is authentic since the reliability and precision of Maalik ad-Daar is not known, and these are the two principle conditions necessary for the authenticity of any narration, as is affirmed in the science of *hadeeth*. Ibn Abee Haatim mentions him in *al-Jarh wat-Ta'deel* (4/1/213) and does not mention anyone who narrates from him except Aboo Saalih. So this indicates that he is unknown, and this is further emphasised by the fact that Ibn Abee Haatim himself, who is well known for his memorisation and wide knowledge, did not quote anyone who declared him reliable, so he remains unknown. Then this does not contradict the saying of al-Haafidh: "... with an authentic chain of narration, from the narration of Aboo Saalih as-Samaan..." since we say: It is not declaration that all of the chain of narration is authentic (*saheeh*), rather only that it is so up to Aboo Saalih. If that were not the case then he would not have started mentioning the chain of narration from Aboo Saalih. Rather he would have begun: "From Maalik ad-Daar... and its chain of narration is authentic." But he said it in the way that he did to draw attention to the fact that there was something requiring investigation in it. The scholars say this for various reasons. From these reasons is that they may not have been able to find a biography for some narrator(s) and therefore they would not permit themselves to pass a ruling on the whole chain of narration. If they had done so it would have meant that they would be passing a ruling of authenticity without certainty and cause others to think it authentic and to use it as a proof. So what they would rather do in such a case is to quote the part

121

requiring further examination, which is what al-Haafidh, *rahimahullaah*, did here. It is also as if he indicates the fact that Aboo Saalih as-Samaan is alone in reporting it from Maalik ad-Daar, or that he is unknown, and Allaah knows best. So this is a very fine point of knowledge which will be realised only by those having experience in this field. What we have said is also aided by the fact that al-Haafidh al-Mundhiree reports another story from the narration of Maalik ad-Daar, from 'Umar in *at-Targheeb* (2/41-41) and says after it: "at-Tabaraanee reports it in *al-Kabeer*. Its narrators up to Maalik ad-Daar are famous and reliable, but as for Maalik ad-Daar then I do not know him." The same is said by al-Haithumee in *Majma' uz-Zawaaid* (3/125). However this point has escaped the author of the book *at-Tawassul* (p.241) so he was deceived by what is apparent from the words of al-Haafidh and he therefore declared the *hadeeth* to be authentic and said in conclusion: "So it mentions only: A man came..." and he says that the narration naming the man as Bilaal ibn al-Haarith is reported by Sayf, whose (weak) condition is known.

But there is no real benefit to be gained from this, rather the whole narration is itself weak due to the fact that Maalik ad-Daar is unknown, as we have shown.

2 . This story is contrary to what is established in the *Sharee'ah* with regard to the prescription of the Rain-Prayer (*Salaatul-Istisqaa*) to seek the sending down of rain. This is reported in many *ahaadeeth*, and it is acted upon

by the vast majority of the scholars. Indeed this story contradicts even what is shown in an *Aayah* of the Qur'aan, that in such circumstances one should supplicate and seek forgiveness, as occurs in the Saying of Allaah, the Most High:

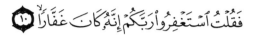

"I (i.e. Nooh) said (to them), 'Ask forgiveness from your Lord; Verily, He is Oft-Forgiving; He will send rain to you in abundance.'"[124]

This was what 'Umar ibn al-Khattaab did when he sought rain using the supplication of al-'Abbaas as a means of *tawassul*, as has preceded. This was also the practice of the Pious Predecessors, whenever they suffered drought they would pray and supplicate, and it is not reported from a single one of them at all that he went to the grave of the Prophet (ﷺ) and requested him to supplicate for rain for them. So if this were something prescribed then they would have done it at least once, so when it is the case that they did not do it, then this shows that what is reported in this story is not something prescribed.

3. Even if the report of the story were authentic there would still be no proof in it for them since the man in the story is himself not named, and therefore unknown. The fact that he is named as Bilaal ibn al-Haarith in the narration of Sayf is worthless since Sayf is Sayf ibn 'Umar at-Tameemee, and the scholars of *hadeeth* are agreed that he is weak. Indeed Ibn Hibbaan says about him: "He reports fabricated things from reliable narrators, and they say that he used to fabricate *hadeeth*." So the narrations of such a person are not acceptable in any case especially when they contradict other reports.

---

124. Soorah Nooh (71): 10-11

NOTE: This person Sayf ibn 'Umar at-Tameemee, is often mentioned in the works of history by at-Tabaree and Ibn Katheer and others, so those who work in the field of history should not neglect to notice his condition, so that they do not give his narrations more credence than they deserve. Similar to him is Loot Yahyaa, Aboo Mikhnaf. Adh-Dhahabee said about him in *al-Meezaan*: "A narrator of historical reports, he is worthless and cannot be relied upon." Aboo Haatim and others declared him to be abandoned. Ad-Daaraqutnee declared him weak. Yahyaa ibn Ma'een said: "He is not at all reliable." Ibn 'Adiyy said: "A fanatical *shee'ee* and reporter of their historical reports." Also like him is Muhammad ibn 'Umar, known as al-Waaqidee, the Shaikh of Ibn Sa'd, the author of *at-Tabaqaat* who narrates a great deal from him. Dr. al-Bootee was beguiled into accepting him and reporting many things from him in *Fiqhus-Seerah* even though he laid down in his introduction that he would only report that which was authentic and reported in reliable books! But al-Waaqidee is someone who is abandoned (*matrook*) in *hadeeth* as had been said by the scholars of *hadeeth*, so be aware.

THE DIFFERENCE BETWEEN *TAWASSUL* BY MEANS OF THE PROPHETS (ﷺ) PERSON AND REQUESTING HIM TO MAKE SUPPLICATION

4 . There is no mention in this report of any *tawassul* by means of the Prophet's (ﷺ) person, rather all it contains is a request for him to supplicate that Allaah, the Most High, should send rain down for the *Ummah*, and this is a separate issue not covered by the preceding *hadeeth*. Nor has anyone from the scholars of the Pious Predecessors, *radiyallaahu 'anhum*, ever declared it to be permissible, i.e. that one may request anything from him after his (ﷺ) death. Shaikhul-Islaam Ibn Taimiyyah said in *al-Qaa'idatul-Jaliyyah* (p.19-20): "Neither the Prophet (ﷺ) nor any of the prophets before him prescribed that the people should supplicate to the angels, the prophets or the pious, nor that they should ask them to intercede for them, neither after their death, nor when they were absent. So nobody says: 'O angel of Allaah intercede with Allaah for me, ask Allaah to grant us victory, or provide or to guide us.' Likewise nobody should say to those prophets or pious people who have died: 'O

prophet of Allaah, O one beloved to Allaah, supplicate to Allaah for me, ask Allaah for me, request Allaah that He should forgive me...' nor should anyone say to them: 'I complain to you of my sins, my loss in provision, or that the enemy has overcome us,' or: 'I complain to you about the person who has oppressed me,' nor 'I have descended in your company, I am your guest, I am your neighbour, or you grant protection to those who request it from you.' Nor should anyone write a request on a piece of paper and place it upon the graves, nor should anyone write a statement that he has taken the protection of so and so, and then use that with the people, as is done by the innovators from the people of the Book and the Muslims, as the Christians do in their churches, and as the innovators do amongst the Muslims at the graves of the prophets and the pious, or in their absence. These are things about which it is known by necessity from the religion of *Islaam,* by *mutawaatir* reports, and by *ijmaa'* of the Muslims, that none of the prophets before him prescribed any of this. Nor did anyone from the Companions of the Prophet (ﷺ), nor any of those who followed them upon good do any of these actions, nor did anyone from the scholars of *Islaam,* neither the four famous *imaams* nor anyone else, declare any of these practices to be recommended. Neither did any of the scholars write that in the rites of *Hajj,* nor at any other time, is it recommend-ed for anyone to make request of the Prophet (ﷺ) at his grave, nor that any-one should ask him to intercede for them, nor that they should ask him to sup-plicate for his *Ummah,* nor should anyone complain to him of any misfortune afflicting the Muslims in their worldly life or their religion. Indeed the Companions suffered various types of trials and afflictions after his death. Sometimes they suffered from drought, sometimes from lack of sustenance, sometimes from fear and strength of an enemy, sometimes they suffered trials due to sins, yet none of them ever went to the grave of the Messenger (ﷺ), nor the grave of Ibraaheem al-Khaleel, nor to the grave of any Prophet and said: 'We complain to you of drought, or strength of the enemy, or the sins we commit.' Nor did anyone say: 'Ask Allaah, for us, or for your *Ummah,* that He should grant them provision, or grant them victory, or forgive them.' Rather all this and its like are from the newly-invented innovations, which are not recommended by anyone at all from the scholars of the Muslims. So these are things which are neither obligatory, nor recommended, by agreement of the scholars of the Muslims, and every innovation which is not obligatory, nor recommended then it is an evil innovation and misguidance by agreement of the Muslims.[125] So anyone who says about any of the innovations that they are 'good innovations', then that can only be said if there is proof in the *Sharee'ah* showing that they are recommended. As for that which is neither recommended nor obligatory, then no one from the Muslims says that such things are good deeds which will draw a person closer to Allaah. Anyone who seeks to draw closer to Allaah with things which are not good deeds, i.e. those which have been ordered by an obligation or a recommendation, then such a one is astray and is following Satan. His way is one of the ways of Satan. Just as 'Abdullaah ibn Mas'ood, *radiyallaahu 'anhu*, said: "Allaah's Messenger (ﷺ) drew a straight line for us, and drew lines to its right and its left, then he said: *This is the way of Allaah, and these are the other ways. Upon each one of these other ways there is a devil calling to it*, then he recited:

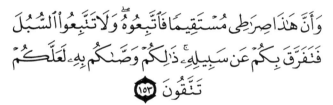

"And verily, this is my Straight Path, so follow it, and follow not (other) paths, for they will separate you away

---

125. The saying of Shaikhul-Islaam has to be taken to mean either (i) That he is addressing the adversaries with what they hold, i.e. that innovations are divided up in accordance with the *Sharee'ah* rulings, from which are obligations and recommendations, or (ii) That he is referring to those things termed to be innovations in the language sense only, which is those things which came about after the Prophet(ﷺ), but which have a proof in the *Sharee'ah* to support them. We say this since it is well-known from him, *rahimahullaah*, that he himself held everything which was an innovation in the *Sharee'ah* to be misguidance, and this is also indicated by the completion of his speech here.

from His Path. This He has ordained for you that you may become *al-Muttaqoon* (the Pious)."126"

Some of the late-comers have fallen into this clear error because they make analogy between the life of the prophets in the *barzakh* (the state between death and the Resurrection) and their lives in this world. But this is a futile analogy contrary to the Book, the *Sunnah*, and reality. A sufficient example for the time being is that no one from the Muslims allows Prayer to be said behind them whilst they are in their graves, nor is anyone able to hold a conversation with them, nor to speak to them, and all the rest of the differences which will not be hidden from a person with intellect.

CALLING UPON OTHERS BESIDES ALLAAH, THE MOST HIGH, FOR ASSISTANCE

This false and futile analogy leads them to the grave misguidance, and disastrous affliction that many of the common Muslims, and some of their elite, have fallen into, and it is the practice of calling upon the prophets and the pious besides Allaah, the Most High, at times of distress and hardship. Indeed you may even hear numerous groups of people standing at graves and calling upon their occupants for help in their various needs. They behave as if those dead people can hear their words, and they ask them for all sorts of needs, in different languages. So in the view of those who call upon them, they know all languages of the world and can distinguish each one from the others, even when people are speaking different languages at the same time! Indeed this is *shirk* with regard to Allaah, the Most High's, attributes, and many people are ignorant of it, and therefore fall into the gravest misguidance. This practice is rebutted and nullified by many *Aayaat*; from them is the Saying of Allaah, the Most High:

---

126. Soorah Al-An'aam (6): 153

$$قُلِ ادْعُوا الَّذِينَ زَعَمْتُم مِّن دُونِهِ فَلَا يَمْلِكُونَ كَشْفَ الضُّرِّ عَنكُمْ وَلَا تَحْوِيلًا ۝$$

"Say (O Muhammad ﷺ): 'Call unto those besides Him - whom you pretend [to be gods like angels, 'Isa (Jesus),' 'Uzair (Ezra) etc]. They have neither the power to remove the adversity from you nor even to shift it from you to another person.'"[127]

Indeed there are many *Aayaat* about this, and a large number of books and treatise have been written in explanation of it.[128] So anyone who has any doubt about this matter, then he should refer to these books and the truth will become clear to him, if Allaah wills. I have come across some quotations from some of the *Hanafee* scholars which I think will be beneficial if quoted here, so that no one may think that what we have said is something not held by the Companions of the well-known *madhhabs*.

Ash-Shaikh Abut-Tayyib Shamsul-Haqq al-'Azeemabaadee said in *Al-Ta'leeq al-Mughnee 'alaa Sunanid-Daaraqutnee* (pp.520-521):

"From the vilest of evil acts and the greatest of innovations and the most severe inventions is the practice of the people of innovation that they mention Shaikh 'Abdul-Qaadir al-Jeelaanee, *rahimahullaah*, by saying: 'O Shaikh 'Abdul-Qaadir al-Jeelaanee grant us something for the sake of Allaah,' and they misdirect their prayers to Baghdad, and many other practices.

---

127. Soorah Al-Israa (17): 56
128. From them is *Qaa'idah Jaliyyah fit-Tawassul wal-waseelah* and *ar-Radd 'alal Bakree* by Shaikhul-Islaam Ibn Taimiyyah, and one of the most comprehensive is *Majmoo'atut-Tawheed an-Najdiyyah* which you should read.

These people are worshippers of others besides Allaah and they make a totally deficient and unjust estimate of Allaah. These ignorant people do not know that the Shaikh, *rahimahullaah*, is not able to bring them an atoms weight of good, nor to remove an atoms weight of evil from them. Why do they call upon him for help and why do they seek their needs from him?![129] Is Allaah not sufficient for His servants?! O Allaah we seek Your refuge from associating anything with You, or honouring any of Your creation with the honour due to You."

They also state in *al-Bazzaaziyyah* and other books of religious rulings: "Whoever claims that the souls of the Shaikhs are present, and that they know what occurs, has become an Unbeliever."[130]

Also ash-Shaikh Fakhruddeen Aboo Sa'd 'Uthmaan al-Jiyaanee ibn Sulaymaan al-Hanafee said in a treatise of his: "Whoever thinks that any dead person has any control over the affairs besides Allaah, and he believes that, then he is an Unbeliever." This is what is mentioned in *Al-Bahrur-Raaiq*. al-Qaadee Hameeduddeen Naakoree al-Hindee said in *at-Tawsheeh*: "From them are those who supplicate to the prophets and the pious when they have a need or are in distress, believing that their spirits are present and hear their call and know of their needs. This is vile *shirk* and clear ignorance, Allaah, the Most High, says:

---

129. Translator's note: See *Soorah az-Zumar: Aayah* 36.
130. *Al-Bahr* (5/134).

$$وَمَنْ أَضَلُّ مِمَّن يَدْعُوا۟ مِن دُونِ ٱللَّهِ مَن$$
$$لَّا يَسْتَجِيبُ لَهُۥٓ إِلَىٰ يَوْمِ ٱلْقِيَٰمَةِ وَهُمْ عَن دُعَآئِهِمْ غَٰفِلُونَ ۝$$

"And who is more astray than one who calls (invokes) besides Allaah, such as will not answer him till the Day of Resurrection, and who are (even) unaware of their calls (invocations) to them?"[131]"

In *al-Bahr* (3/94) there occurs: "If such a person marries, attesting his belief in Allaah and His Messenger, then the marriage is not correct. Rather he is an Unbeliever due to his belief that the prophet (ﷺ) knows the Hidden and Unseen."[132]

Its like occurs in the *Fataawaa* of Qaadee Khaan, al-'Aynee, *ad-Durrul-Mukhtaar*, *al-'Aalamgeeriyyah* and other books by the *Hanafee* scholars, Then as for the Noble *Aayaat* and sayings in the pure *Sunnah* in refutation of the foundations of *shirk*, and in pure rebuke of those guilty of it, then they are too many to be counted. Our Shaikh, the scholar, as-Sayyid Muhammad Nadheer Husayn ad-Dehlawee has a clear and beneficial treatise in reply to these evil innovations."

---

131. Soorah Al-Ahqaaf (46): 5

132. Similar to this is the common practice of many people that they answer questions by saying: "Allaah and His Messenger know best"! Since what is reported in that regard as the saying of some of the companions, then it was during his lifetime. But after his death that is not permissible at all. (i.e. one should just say "Allaah knows best.")

The Second Report: The report about making an opening to the sky about the grave of Allaah's Messenger (ﷺ).

Ad-Daarimee reports in his *Sunan* (1/43): Abun-Nu'maan narrated to us: Sa'eed ibn Zayd narrated to us: 'Amr ibn Maalik an-Nukree narrated to us: Abul-Jawzaa Aws ibn 'Abdullaah narrated to us, saying: "The people of al-Madeenah suffered a very severe drought, so they complained to 'Aaishah, so she said: "See the grave of the Prophet(ﷺ), make an opening in the roof above it, so that there is nothing between it and the sky." He said: So they did so, and we were blessed with rain such that the crops grew and camels became fat and swollen, so it was called the year of increase."

This chain of narration is weak and cannot be used as a proof due to three reasons:

(i) Sa'eed ibn Zayd who is the brother of Hammaad ibn Zayd is somewhat weak. Al-Haafidh said about him in *at-Taqreeb*: "Generally acceptable, but he makes mistakes." Adh-Dhahabee said about him in *al-Meezaan*: "Yahyaa ibn Sa'eed said: 'weak', and as-Sa'dee said: 'He is not a proof, they declare his *ahaadeeth* to be weak.' An-Nasaa'ee and others said: 'He is not strong' and Ahmad said: 'He is all right.' Yahyaa ibn Sa'eed would not accept him."

(ii) It is *mawqoof*, coming only from 'Aaishah and not from the Prophet (ﷺ), and even if the chain of narration upto 'Aaishah were authentic then it would not be a proof since it is something open to personal judgement in which even the Companions are sometimes correct and sometimes incorrect, and we are not bound to act upon that.

(iii) That the Abun-Nu'maan in its *isnaad* is Muhammad ibn al-Fadl, who is known as 'Aarim'. He was originally a reliable narrator except that he deteriorated at the end of his life. Al-Haafidh Burhaanud-Deen al-Halabee mentions him amongst those who deteriorated in later life in his book: *al-Muqaddimah* (p.391) and he says: "The ruling about these people is that the narrations of these people are accepted if reported from them by people who heard from them before they deteriorated. But narrations reported from them by those who heard from them after they deteriorated, or narrations reported from them by people about whom we do not know whether they heard from them before they deteriorated or after, then these narrations are to be rejected."

I say: We do not know whether this report was heard by ad-Daarimee from him before or after his memory deteriorated, so it is therefore not acceptable, and cannot be used as evidence.[133]

Then Shaikhul-Islaam Ibn Taimiyyah said in *ar-Radd 'alal-Bakree* (pp68-74): "What is reported from 'Aaishah, *radiyallaahu 'anhaa*, that an opening was made above his grave to the sky, in order for rain to be sent down, then that is not authentic. Its chain of narration is not reliable, and a clear proof of its being a lie is the fact that no such opening existed above the house at all in the whole of the life of 'Aaishah. Rather it remained as it had been in the time of the Prophet (ﷺ), part of it being covered and a part uncovered. The sun used to shine into it as is established in the two *Saheehs* from 'Aaishah that the Prophet (ﷺ) used to pray the *'Asr* Prayer whilst the sun was shining into her house and not producing shade. Then the room remained like that attached to the mosque of the Messenger (ﷺ)... then the Prophetic room was entered into the mosque. Then a high wall was built around the room of 'Aaishah, which contained the grave. Then after that a window was built in the roof so that it was possible to enter through it if there was a need to sweep it clean. But as for the presence of such an opening during the lifetime of 'Aaishah, then it is a clear lie. Even if that were true then it would only be a proof that the people had not used to seek from Allaah by means of the right of a created being, and that they had not used to make *tawassul* in their supplication by means of a deceased person, nor ask Allaah through him. Rather they opened up an opening above the grave so that mercy should descend upon it. They did not make any supplication by means of his right, so what is the connection between this

---

133. Ash-Shaikh al-Ghumaaree missed this weakness in *al-Misbaah* (p.43), just as it was ignored by another in order to give the impression to the people that this report is authentic.

and that?!

"So a created being can only benefit another by means of his supplication or his action. So Allaah, the Most High, loves that we seek nearness to Him by means of *eemaan*, righteous actions, by sending prayers for blessings upon His Prophet (ﷺ), by our loving him, obeying him and allying ourselves with him. These are the things which Allaah loves us to seek nearness to Him by means of. If people think that we are to seek nearness to Him merely by means of people who are loved by Allaah, and not by our doing anything which Allaah loves us to do in order to draw nearer to Him, such as *Eemaan* and righteous actions, then this idea is false and futile, as shown both by the intellect and the *Sharee'ah*. As for the intellect, then the mere fact that a particular person is loved by Allaah in no way means or necessitates that my need will be fulfilled by my making *tawassul* by means of his person, if neither I nor he do anything which is a cause for the fulfilment of my need. If however he supplicates for me, or I have *eemaan* in him (ﷺ) and do actions of obedience to him, then there is no doubt that this is a means of nearness. But what means of nearness (*waseelah*) is there for me in the person beloved to Allaah, if I do not do anything that is required of me with regard to him, such as would produce such a result.

"As for the *Sharee'ah*, then it is that all worship is based upon following the Messenger (ﷺ), not in innovating new practices. So no one has the right to prescribe anything in the religion if Allaah had not permitted it. So it is not allowed for anyone to pray to his (ﷺ) grave, and then say: He has more right that we should pray towards him than the *Ka'bah*. It is established in the *Saheeh* that he (ﷺ) said: *Do not sit upon graves and do not pray towards them*. Despite this some people who go beyond all bounds pray to the graves of their shaikhs, and even turn their backs on the *Qiblah* and pray instead to the graves, and say : 'This is the *Qiblah* for the chosen worshippers and the *Ka'bah* is the *Qiblah* for the common people'! Other people think that Prayer said near to the graves of their shaikhs is better than prayer in the mosques, better even than Prayer in *al-Masjidul-Haraam* (in Makkaah), *al-Masjidun-Nabawee* (in Madeenah) and *al-Aqsaa* (in Jerusalem). Then many people think that supplicating at the graves of the prophets and the pious is better than supplicating in the mosques. All these are things which are known by everyone who is a scholar of the religion of *Islaam* to be in direct contradiction to the *Sharee'ah* of *Islaam*. So whoever does not cling with regard to these matters and all matters, to the Book and the *Sunnah,* then he has strayed into misguidance and into misguiding others, and has fallen into the abyss of destruction. So the servant must submit totally to the perfect, pure and clear *Sharee'ah* brought by Muhammad (ﷺ), and must agree that it brings everything good and does so to perfection, and that it removes all harm. So then if he sees any forms of worship or devotions and so on which people think are good and beneficial, but these are not things prescribed in the *Sharee'ah*, then he knows for certain that their harm outweighs any benefit in them, and their evil outweighs any good, since the *Sharee'ah* does not leave out anything beneficial at all." Then he said: "And supplication is one of the greatest forms of worship, so a person should stick to the prescribed supplications, since they are preserved from any sin, just as in all other forms of worship they should be performed in the manner laid down in the *Sharee'ah*, for this is the Straight Path, and may Allaah, the Most High, grant us and the rest of our brothers, the Believers, success."

NOTE: This book of ad-Daarimee is written in the manner of the four *Sunan,* in the arrangement of its books and chapters, therefore what is correct is that it is described as: '*as-Sunan*', as it was called by the noble Shaikh Dahmaan in his printed version of it. It was formerly known famously as *Musnadud-Daarimee* and this is a mistake having no basis from the scholars. An even bigger mistake is to describe it with the term *as-Saheeh* and this is not correct at all since it contains many *marfoo' ahaadeeth* whose chain of narrations are weak, and also some have one or more missing links, others are *mawqoof*[134]

---

134. Reports from the sayings of the Companions.

reports, many of which are weak as is the case with the report in question here. So how can the book be described as 'as-Saheeh'!! A similar mistake is the use of the term 'the authentic (saheeh) books' to refer to the four Sunan, as some people term them! This is not only contrary to their true titles as-Sunan, but it is also contrary to reality, since they also contain many weak ahaadeeth. It is also contrary to what their authors did, i.e. that they themselves sometimes indicated weak ahaadeeth within their books, particularly Imaam at-Tirmidhee who explained the weakness of many ahaadeeth in his book. In Sunan Ibn Maajah there are a number of fabricated narrations, not to mention weak ahaadeeth, so only an ignorant person or someone with personal gain at stake would refer to the Sunan books as 'the authentic (Saheeh) books.'

• *the fourth doubt*
MAKING ANALOGY BETWEEN THE CREATOR AND THE CREATION

The adversaries say: *Tawassul* by means of the persons of the Pious, and by means of their honour is something desirable and permissible since it is based upon rational thinking. This is because if one of us needs something from a king, or a minister, or a person in a position of authority, then he does not go to him directly, since he is aware that his request would probably not be given any attention, assuming that he is not turned away immediately. Therefore it is quite natural for him, when he wants something from such a person, that he should seek someone who knows him, someone close to him who carries some weight with him, and make that person an intermediary with him. If that is done then the person will receive an answer and achieve what he desires. Then they claim: The case is just the same with regard to our connection with Allaah, the One free of any defect or blemish, since Allaah is the Mightiest of the Mighty, the Greatest and Most Proud, whereas we are disobedient sinners and therefore very far from Allaah, so it is not fitting that we call upon Him directly. If we were to do so then we would be afraid that He would reject us outright, or at least not give any attention to us so that we would return with nothing. But there are pious people such as prophets, the messengers and the martyrs who are nearer to Allaah, the One free of all imperfections, and He will respond to them if they call upon Him, and He will accept their intercession if they intercede for anyone. So, they say, should we not then use their honour as a means of nearness (*tawassul*) to Him, and begin our supplication by mentioning their names. Hopefully Allaah will listen to us because of their honourable status with Him, and therefore answer our supplications. So why, they say, do people prevent this form of *tawassul* when it is something which the people use between themselves, why can they not do the same with regard to the Lord whom they worship?

We say in reply to this doubt: What you are doing therefore is making analogy between the Creator and the creation. You imagine there to be similarity between the One who sustains the Heavens and the Earth, the Judge of judges, the Most Just, the extremely Merciful and Mercy-Giving, and those oppressive rulers, those tyrannical kings who do not care at all for the well-being of their subjects, those who place hindrances and barriers between themselves and their subjects, who do not allow anyone to approach them except by means of intermediaries whom you have to bribe and give gifts to, you have to submit and humiliate yourself to them, you have to gain their approval and cause them to be happy with you. So O unfortunate people, had it ever crossed your minds that when you do this you are slandering your Lord, accusing Him, committing injustice towards Him, and describing Him with that which He hates and which displeases Him?

Has it not crossed your minds that you are describing Allaah, the Most High, with the most ugly attributes when you make analogy between Him and the oppressive rulers, and wicked kings? How does your religion allow you to do this? How does this conform with the fact that it is obligatory upon you to honour your Lord and declare the praises of your Creator? So do you not see that if it were possible for the people to address the ruler face to face, and that they were able to speak with him directly without intermediary, then that would be more perfect and praiseworthy for him, rather than when he can only be addressed by means of intermediaries who may make the affair harder or easier as they please?

O people, when you give speeches you are very proud of 'Umar ibn al-Khattaab and you praise him and commend him, and you explain to the people that he was a very humble person, and not at all proud or haughty, and that he was always close to the people. The weakest of them could come to him and speak to him without any intermediary or anyone to gain admission for them. Then he would examine their need and grant it to them if they had a right. Do you not think that this style of authority is better and more excellent, or the type which you make as an example of you Lord? What is wrong with you? How do you judge? What has happened to your intellect? Where has it gone? Where has sound thinking disappeared to, and how can you allow yourselves to make a similarity between Allaah, the Most High, and a tyrannical king? Or how is it that Satan has led you to make analogy between Allaah, the One free of every blemish and defect, and an oppressive ruler? O people, if you had made a similarity between Allaah, the Most High, and the most pious people, and the best of them, then you would be guilty of Unbelief (*Kufr*), then how about when you make a similarity between Him, the Most Perfect, and the most tyrannical, wicked and depraved of people?

O people if you had made analogy between your Majestic Lord and 'Umar ibn al-Khattaab, the pious and just, then you would have fallen into *shirk*, so how has Satan led you to such a state that you are only satisfied when he has led you to make analogy between your Lord and the oppressive and corrupt kings, rulers and ministers? Indeed taking Allaah, the Most High, to be like His creation is Unbelief (*Kufr*) whatever the case, and He, the One free of all imperfections, warns against it, Saying:

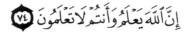

"And they worship others besides Allaah, such as do not and can not own any provision for them from the heavens or the earth. So put not forward similitudes for Allaah (as there is nothing similar to Him, nor does He resemble anything). Truly Allaah knows and you know not."[135]

Just as He, the One free of every defect and blemish, denies any likeness between Him and anything from His Creation, as He says:

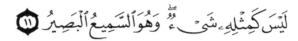

"There is nothing like unto Him, and He is the All-Hearer, the All-Seer"[136]

The worst similarity a person can make is that he imagines Him to be like the evil, wicked and corrupt rulers, thinking that he is doing something good! Indeed it is this which causes some of the scholars to be very severe and harsh in reprimanding *tawassul* by means of the persons of the prophets. This is why they declare it to amount to *shirk* even if the action itself is not in our view *shirk*. But it is to be feared greatly that it will lead to *shirk*, and indeed that is exactly what it has done in the case of those who seek to justify their *tawassul* by means of this similarity, which is itself Unbelief (*Kufr*), if only they knew. At this point it will become clear that the saying of one of the Islamic callers today, in principle number fifteen of his twenty principles: "If supplication is joined with *tawassul* to Allaah by means of one of His creation, then this is merely a minor difference relating to the manners of supplication, and it is not from the

---

135. Soorah An-Nahl (16): 73-74
136. Soorah Ash-Shooraa (42): 11

affairs of *'aqeedah* (creed/belief)," is not correct unrestrictedly, as you have seen that in reality it is a disagreement relating to fundamental matters, since it leads to clear *shirk* as has preceded. Perhaps the like of this saying which causes people to be lax about this deviation is one of the reasons which prevent people from researching this matter and seeking the truth about it, which results in the end in allowing the innovators to continue upon their innovation, and allows it to grow in its seriousness and danger. Therefore Imaam al-'Izz ibn 'Abdis-Salaam said in his treatise: *Al-Waasitah* (p.5): "Whoever makes the prophets, and the scholars of the religion, intermediaries between Allaah and His creation, like the door keepers employed by earthly kings who come between them and their subjects, and thinks that they are the ones who raise up the needs of the creation to Allaah, the Most High, and that Allaah, the Most High, guides, gives provision and aid to His creation through them, meaning that the creation make request of them and then they in turn make request of Allaah, just as the intermediaries with earthly kings pass on the request of subjects to them, and the people ask them since it is not deemed correct for them to ask the king directly, and it is more beneficial for them to make their request to the intermediaries than to ask the king directly, since they are closer to the king. So whoever deems them to be intermediaries **in this way**, then he is a *Kaafir* and a *mushrik*. His repentance is to be sought, and he either repents or he is killed. Such people make similarity with Allaah; they take Him to be like His creation, and attribute rivals to Allaah..."

● *t h e   f i f t h   d o u b t*
IS THERE ANYTHING TO PREVENT THE INNOVATED *TAWASSUL* BEING-MERELY SOMETHING PERMISSIBLE BUT NOT AS SOMETHING RECOMMENDED ?

Someone may say: It is correct that there is nothing established in the *Sunnah* which is an evidence to show the recommendation of *tawassul* by means of the persons of the prophets and the pious, but what is there to prevent us if we do it merely as something that is permissible for us, since there is no forbiddance of it reported?

This is a futile doubt which we have heard from some people who wish to take a middle position between the two sides, in order to please them both and to avoid being accused by either of them! Then the reply is: We must not forget here what the meaning of *Waseelah* is, which is that by means of which some goal is attained, as has preceded. Then the goal which we wish to arrive at will either be religious or worldly. So if the first is the case, then it is not possible to know the means that will attain the religious goal except by way of the *Sharee'ah*. So if a man claimed for example that he was going to use one of the great signs of Allaah, the Most High, in His creation, such as the night and the day, and that it was a reason for his supplication to be answered. Then that would be rejected unless he brought a proof for it, and he could not merely say that it was a permissible form of *tawassul*. That would be a self-contradictory statement since he calls it '*tawassul*' and this has not been established in the *Sharee'ah*, and he has no other way of affirming it. This is different to the second of the two cases, i.e. worldly affairs, since worldly means can be known by means of the intellect, or through knowledge or experience and so on. Like a man who does business by selling wine. This is a known way of attaining wealth, so it is a way of attaining the goal of amassing wealth. However this is a means which Allaah has prohibited, so it is forbidden to sell it, as opposed to the case if he traded in something which Allaah - the Mighty and Majestic - has forbidden, then it would be lawful. But as for something which it is claimed is a means of drawing nearer to Allaah, and that it causes ones supplication to be more acceptable - then this cannot be known except by means of the *Sharee'ah*. So when it is said: This is not found in the *Sharee'ah*, it is not permissable even to call it a '*waseelah*' nor then to follow that by saying that it is permissable to use it as a means of tawassul. This has been spoken about in detail in the second chapter of this book.

A second matter is that this *tawassul* which we have agreed is not found in the *Sharee'ah* - while there is in the *Sharee'ah* that which will fully suffice us so that we have no need of it. So what can cause the Muslim to prefer this *tawassul* which is not found in the *Sharee'ah*, and turn away from the *tawassul* which is found in the *Sharee'ah*? All of the scholars are agreed that if an innovation clashes with a sunnah, then it is an innovation of misguidance, and this *tawassul* is like that - so it is not permissable to use it, not even as something which is not recommended, but as something permitted!

A third matter is that *tawassul* by means of peoples persons resembles the *tawassul* which people do by means of an intermediaries to their earthly kings and rulers. Whereas there is nothing like Allaah - the Blessed and the Most High - as is agreed to even by those who perform that *tawassul*. So if the Muslim performs *tawassul* to Him - the Most High - by means of persons, then in his action he has made a resemblance between Him and those kings and rulers - as has been explained, and that is not permissable.

* *t h e   s i x t h   d o u b t*

MAKING ANALOGY BETWEEN *TAWASSUL* BY MEANS OF THE PERSON OR STATUS OF SOMEBODY AND *TAWASSUL* BY MEANS OF RIGHTEOUS ACTIONS

This is a further doubt raised by those innovators[137], it has been make alluring for them by Satan, and he has lead them to say: "You have stated that from the prescribed forms of *tawassul* by agreement, is *tawassul* to Allaah, the Most High, by means of righteous actions. So if this *tawassul* is permissible then *tawassul* by means of the righteous person who did the action has even more right that it should be declared permissible. It has even more right that it should be prescribed, and it should not be criticised." Then the reply is from two angles:

1 .   This is a case of analogy and analogy with regard to forms of worship is futile as has preceded, and the example of the person who says this saying is just the same as one who says: If it is permissible for a person to make *tawassul* by means of his own righteous actions, which are without doubt less than

---

137. From them is the author of *at-Taaj*.

the actions of the pious ones loved by Allaah, and the Prophet, then it is permissible for him to make *tawassul* by means of the actions of the prophet and the pious. So this and whatever follows on from it is false and futile.

2 . This is a clear error, since we do not say, and neither has any of the Pious Predecessors before us said, that it is permissible for the Muslims to make *tawassul* by means of the righteous actions of another person. Rather the *tawassul* which is indicated is *tawassul* by means of the persons own righteous actions. So when this is clear we turn their previous saying around upon them and say: when it is not permissible to perform *tawassul* by means of righteous actions done by someone other than the person making the supplication, then it is even more certain and fitting that it is not permissible to make *tawassul* by means of his person. This is not difficult to see, and all praise and thanks are for Allaah.

• *t h e   s e v e n t h   d o u b t*
MAKING ANALOGY BETWEEN *TAWASSUL* BY MEANS OF THE PROPHET'S (ﷺ) PERSON AND SEEKING BENEFIT

This is a further doubt which was not known in the centuries that have passed, but it was invented and given currency by Dr. Bootee himself, since he affirms in his book: *Fiqhus-Seerah* (pp.344-355) whilst discussing the lessons to be learnt from what occurred at Hudaibiyyah, that it shows the prescription of seeking benefit from things left behind by the Prophet (ﷺ). Then he makes analogy between that and between *tawassul* by means of his person after his death. He comes to a very strange and surprising conclusion as a result of that, which is something that has not been said by anyone who occupies himself with knowledge, not even those who are drowned in blind-following, clinging to their own views stubbornly, and innovating in the religion. To prevent anyone thinking that we are oppressing him by attributing things to him which he did not say, we will quote his own words completely, and we apologise to the readers because of its length. He said: "When you know that *tabarruk* is seeking benefit by means of something and through it, then you will know that *tawassul* by means of the traces left behind of the Prophet(ﷺ) is something recommended and prescribed. Not to mention *tawassul* by means of his noble person. There is no difference in that between when he (ﷺ) was alive and after his death, since his traces and those things which he left behind, are not something living; seeking benefit from them or *tawassul* by means of them is thus the same in his lifetime or after his death. The Companions sought to make *tawassul* by means of his hairs after his death, as is confirmed in *Saheehul-Bukhaaree* in the chapter of the grey-hairs of Allaah's Messenger(ﷺ), and they deny *tawassul* by means of his (ﷺ) person after his death, since they say that the effect of the Prophet (ﷺ) ceased with his death, so *tawassul* by means of him is *tawassul* by means of something having no effect at all. This is a proof which only shows an amazing level of ignorance, since it is established with regard to the Messenger of Allaah (ﷺ) that he had a personal influence and effect upon the affairs in his lifetime, such as would necessitate that we research and see what happened to this influence and effect after his death? No person from the Muslims can attribute to anyone that they in person have an influence and effect upon any affair, except the One, Single Lord. Whoever believes something different to this then he is an Unbeliever BY CONSENSUS OF ALL THE MUSLIMS. So the reason behind seeking benefit from him, and using him or his traces as a means of *tawassul* is not that he is the cause of any effect, but rather the reason for it is that he is the most excellent of all the creation to Allaah unrestrictedly, and because he is a mercy from Allaah for the people. So it is *tawassul* by means of his (ﷺ) closeness to his Lord, and because of his great mercy towards the creation. In this way the blind-man performed *tawassul* by means of him (ﷺ) so that his sight should be restored, so Allaah restored his sight to him.[138] For this reason and in the same way the Companions used to perform *tawassul* with his traces and things emanating from him without receiving any criticism from him. It

---

138. Dr. al-Bootee mentioned in a footnote to the *hadeeth* of the blind-man that in some narrations there occurs the addition: "So whenever you have a need then do the same"! ignorant of its weakness.

had already preceded that it is recommended to seek intercession from the good and pious people and members of the prophetic household for purposes of seeking rain and vast majority of the Imaams and scholars, amongst them ash-Shawkaanee, Ibn Qudaamah, as-San'aanee and others. To then make distinction about that between his lifetime and the time after his (ﷺ) death is an amazing and very strange mistake and confusion with nothing to permit it."

We have many objections to raise against these words, from the most important of them are the following:

1.   We have previously mentioned al-Bootee's attacks upon the *Salafees* and his accusation that their hearts contain no trace of love for Allaah's Messenger (ﷺ) and his basis for saying that is that they deny *tawassul* by means of him (ﷺ) after his death. This is a futile and false accusation, and an unfair and oppressive slander. There is no doubt that Allaah, the Most High, will take account of him severely if he does not sincerely repent from it. This is because it means a declaration against thousands of Muslims that they are Unbelievers, without any proof or evidence except suspicion and delusion, neither of which are of any benefit in arriving at the truth.

2.   He has jumbled up the truth with falsehood to an amazing degree. Then he uses the truth that he has as proof of the falsehood. Because of this he arrives at an opinion which nobody has ever preceded him in. So if we wish to distinguish between the two types of speech, then we say: The truth contained in his words is:

    (a) That the Prophet (ﷺ) is indeed close to Allaah, the Blessed and the Most High, and he was a mercy from Allaah, the Most High, for the creation.

    (b) That nobody, not even the Prophet (ﷺ) has a personal influence and effect upon the affairs, rather all influence over the affairs is exercised by Allaah, the One and Single Lord.

(c) That it is prescribed to seek benefit from the traces emanating from the Prophet (ﷺ),[139]and that the Companions did
that during his (ﷺ) lifetime and he tacitly approved of that.

These three points are correct and there is no disagreement about them, and
if the author had withheld after this, then there would be no need to com-
ment. As for the falsehood contained in his words, about which there is indeed
great disagreement, then it is:

(a) That it is permissible to make *tawassul* by means of the
traces emanating from the Prophet (ﷺ), and that the
Companions used to make *tawassul* by means of his traces and
what emanated from him.

(b) He makes *tawassul* and *tabarruk* (seeking benefit) one
and the same.

(c) That it is permissible to make *tawassul* by means of his person just as it is permissible to seek benefit from his traces and
things emanating from him.

(d) The reason allowing *tawassul* by means of him (ﷺ) is that
he is the best of all the creation to Allaah.

(e) His ignorance of the meaning of intercession such that he
uses it as a proof for the innovated form of *tawassul*.

---

139. Translators note: e.g. his hair when cut and the water which he used for *wudoo* etc.

(f) He falsely accuses the *Salafees* of claiming that they hold that the Prophet (ﷺ) used to have a personal effect and influence over the affairs in his lifetime, and that this ceased when he died, and that this is why they deny *tawassul* by means of him (ﷺ) after his death.

(g) He claims that the blind man did *tawassul* by means of the Prophet's (ﷺ) nearness to his Lord.

(h) He claims that Muhammad (ﷺ) is the most excellent of all the creation unrestrictedly.

So we will now explain all these points in detail, so we say:

1. AL-BOOTEE'S ERROR IN MAKING *TABARRUK* (SEEKING BENEFIT) AND *TAWASSUL* ONE AND THE SAME.

Dr. Bootee said: "*Tawassul* by means of the traces left by the prophet (ﷺ) is something recommended and prescribed, not to mention *tawassul* by means of his noble person." So it is apparent from his words that he makes analogy between *tawassul* by means of his (ﷺ) person with seeking benefit from traces left by him, and justifies it thereby. He then calls this seeking benefit '*tawassul*', and what we have said is further emphasised by what he says on p.196 of the same book where, after mentioning some reports about the Companions seeking blessings from traces left by him (ﷺ), he says: "So if this is so with regard to *tawassul* by means of his physical traces, then how about *tawassul* by means of his station with Allaah, the Majestic? And how about *tawassul* by means of his being a mercy for the worlds?" But he quickly retreats from this and then claims that seeking blessings and *tawassul* are one and the same, and he denies that he makes analogy between them. So he says: "So do not let yourself make the mistake of thinking that we make analogy between *tawassul* and seeking benefit. This is a question that cannot be resolved by means of analogy, since *tawassul* and *tabarruk* (seeking benefit) are merely two words for the same thing, which is seeking good and blessing by way of the means (*waseelah*). So both *tawassul* by means of his (ﷺ) status with Allaah, and *tawassul* by means of his traces, and what emanates from him, and his clothes, all of these are single examples and parts entering within a comprehensive whole, which is unrestricted *tawassul*, whose ruling is established in the authentic *ahaadeeth*. Then all the individual forms enter under the generality of the text, by means of what is known to the scholars as 'overlooking that which is superfluous'." But in reality what is apparent from his initial words is much less serious than what he says at the end, since *tawassul* is very clearly something totally different from *tabarruk*. Whoever tried to say that they are one and the same has committed a very serious error, and has fallen into grave ignorance of *Sharee'ah* realities, such things as are impermissible for any student of knowledge with self-respect. *Tabarruk* is seeking benefit by a person who gains possession of something from the remnants and traces left by the Prophet (ﷺ) hoping for good through it, as something particular to him (ﷺ). As for *Tawassul*, then it is to accompany ones supplication to Allaah, the Most High, with one of the means of nearness which Allaah, the Most High, has prescribed for His servants. For example that he says: "O Allaah I ask You by means of my love for Your Prophet (ﷺ) that You forgive me" and so on. So the difference can be seen in two things:

(i) That through *tabarruk* one hopes only for worldly good, as opposed to *tawassul* by means of which one may hope for good in either the worldly life or the Hereafter of both.

(ii) *Tabarruk* is a means of seeking immediate benefit and good as has preceded, as opposed to *tawassul* which is merely an accompaniment to ones supplication, it cannot be used except along with supplication.

So in explanation of all this we say: It is prescribed for the Muslim to make *tawassul* when supplicating by means of one of the perfect names of Allaah, the Blessed and Most High, for example, and that through this he seeks to attain the fulfilment of any worldly need, such as increase in provision, or any need relating to the Hereafter, such as being saved from the Fire. So he says: "O Allaah I ask You, and seek nearness to You by the fact that You are Allaah, the One, the Self-Sufficient Master of all, that You cure me," or, "You enter me into Paradise…"

Nobody can criticise this person for any of this. However it is not permissible for the Muslims to do this whilst seeking benefit from something left behind by the Prophet (ﷺ). So he cannot and it is not permissible for him to say, for example: "O Allaah I ask You and use as a means of nearness to You, the robe of Your Prophet, or his shin, or his urine, that You forgive me and have mercy upon me…" Anyone who did the like of this would without a doubt give the people grounds to seriously doubt his sanity and capacity of understanding, not to mention his belief and the state of his religion. What is apparent from the words of Dr. al-Bootee is, however, that he would allow this weird *tawassul*, and that he would consider it and seeking benefit through the traces left by the Prophet (ﷺ) to be one and the same thing. So by this he is not afraid of accusing the *Salafees* of falling into an amazing mistake and confusion for-thinking that there is nothing to permit it. However the readers will now be aware who has truly fallen into blind error and confusion. This reminds us of the piece of Arabian wisdom which says: "She accused me of her own fault and then slipped away." Indeed how truthfully the noble Messenger (ﷺ) said: *From that which the people received from the earlier Prophets is: 'If you do not feel shame then do as you wish.'*[140]

There is a very serious and dangerous point which attention must be drawn to, and that is that he claims that any *tawassul*, without restriction, is affirmed by the authentic *ahaadeeth*. This is false and futile since it is no more than an assumption and a mere claim without any reality, except in his imagination. Rather the only *tawassul* relating to the Prophet (ﷺ) that is established is

---

140. Reported by Ahmad, al-Buhaaree (transl. 8/89/141) and others.

tawassul by means of his (ﷺ) supplication, as has preceded.

As for *tawassul* by means of his (ﷺ) status or the traces he left behind, then nothing at all from that is established in the Book or the *Sunnah*. Indeed we request the Dr. to show us a single authentic *hadeeth* showing what he claims, and we are certain that he will not be able to find any such thing. Indeed we are accustomed to him affirming very serious rulings without the slightest shred of evidence! He also makes very great claims which have no foundation, except that this is how something seems to him. It is sufficient for him that the reader believes and fully accepts whatever he says, but let the reader beware of asking for a proof for anything he says, because that in his view shows bad manners and lack of religion, and is the way of the *Salafees*. So we seek Allaah's refuge. So be aware!

2. THE FALSENESS OF *TAWASSUL* BY MEANS OF THE TRACES LEFT BEHIND BY THE PROPHET(ﷺ)

After establishing the difference between *tawassul* and *tabarruk*, then we will know that we do not seek to use the traces left by the Prophet (ﷺ) as a means of *tawassul* to Allaah, but rather we seek to gain benefit through them only, meaning that by obtaining them we would hope for the attainment of some worldly benefit, as has preceded. We hold that *tawassul* by means of the traces left by the Prophet (ﷺ) has never been something prescribed, and that it is a lie against the Companions, *radiyallaahu 'anhum*, to claim that they used to make *tawassul* with these traces. Whoever wishes to claim something contrary to this then let him bring proof and establish that the Companions used to say in their supplications, for example: "O Allaah, by means of the saliva of Your Prophet, or his excrement, save us from the Fire"!! No sane person would even allow such a thing to be narrated, so how about using such means. Then if Dr. al-Bootee is still in doubt about that, and he thinks that it is permissible, then he should affirm this in practice by supplicating with supplications such as these upon the pulpit. If he does not do it, and he will not do it, if Allaah wills, as long as he remains sane, and as long as a grain of *eemaan* remains in his heart, then that is a proof that he says with his tongue what he does not believe in his heart. We must also draw attention to the fact that we believe in the permissibility of seeking benefit through the traces left by the Prophet (ﷺ) and we do not deny it, contrary to the impression given by our adversary. However seeking to derive benefit has conditions, from them is correct *eemaan* as demanded by the *Sharee'ah* and as is acceptable to Allaah. So one who is not a sincere and true Muslim, then Allaah will not grant him any good by his seeking to desire benefit in this way. A further condition for one desiring to attain such benefits is that he actually obtains a true remnant left by the Prophet (ﷺ) which he then uses for this purpose. But we know that the remnants left by him (ﷺ), whether robes, or hair, or things emanating from him, are now lost to us, and it is not possible for anyone to establish for certain that anything from them remains. Since this is the case then seeking benefit from these remnants is no longer an issue in our time,[141] rather it has become a purely academic question, so it is not fitting that it should be spoken about at great length. However there is a matter which must be explained which is that the Prophet (ﷺ) even though he allowed the Companions in the battle of Hudaybiyyah and at other such times, to seek benefit from and to seek after the traces which he left, then that was for an important reason which was particularly important at that time. This reason was to strike fear in the Unbelievers of Quraysh, and

---

141. The Dr. in question tried in a footnote (p.197) of his aforementioned book to reply to something which I wrote in my treatise *Naqd Nusoos Hadeethiyyah* in reply to al-Khattaanee. He quotes that I said in it: "There is no benefit to be hoped for from the *ahaadeeth* about seeking benefit from the traces left by him (ﷺ) in this age..." It is unfortunate that the Dr. has managed, in this brief quote, to manifest a clear example of treachery in quoting what others say, since he has twisted my words badly, rather what I actually said was: "There is no great benefit in affirming the prescription of seeking benefit from his (ﷺ) traces in our day." So see, may Allaah have mercy upon you, how the Dr. changed and twisted my words. I cannot see that he had any other purpose in doing that except to use it as an excuse to attack me and to incite the common people against me. So do you, O brother reader, think that such behaviour is consistent with piety and fear of Allaah, the Mighty and Majestic, and with a sincere desire to attain the truth? I have fully replied to these lies.., and this has recently appeared in the form of a treatise: *Difaa' 'anil-hadeeth in-Nabawee was-Seerah*...

to show the level of devotion which the Muslims had for their Prophet, and their love of him, and how they dedicated themselves to his service, and the respect they had for him. But it is not permissible to overlook, nor to hide the fact that after this battle the Prophet (ﷺ) encouraged Muslims, with wise means and in every fine manner, to turn away from this means of seeking benefit, and guided them instead to righteous actions which were better for them with Allaah, the Mighty and Majestic, and more profitable. This is shown by the following *hadeeth*: From 'Abdur-Rahmaan ibn Abee Quraad, *radiyallaahu 'anhu*, that the Prophet (ﷺ) made *wudoo* one day and the Companions wiped themselves with the water remaining from his *wudoo*, so the Prophet(*) said to them: *What leads you to do this?* They said: "Love of Allaah and His Messenger." So the Prophet (ﷺ) said: *Whoever is pleased that he should love Allaah and His Messenger, or that Allaah and His Messenger should love him, then let him make his speech truthful, and let him fulfil his trust when he is trusted, and let him behave as a good neighbour.*[142]

3. A SWEEPING SLANDER

It seems that the Dr. cannot enjoy life or have peace of mind unless he invents slanders against the *Salafees*, and lies against them. Sometimes the lies are open and at other times they are covered. So here he invents a slander against us, claiming that we use as a proof to prevent *tawassul* by means of the Prophet (ﷺ), after his death, the saying that his personal influence over affairs ceased after his death, and that it is therefore not correct to make *tawassul* by means of him (ﷺ) after his death. He adds the extra fact that the Prophet (ﷺ) did not have any personal effect over the affairs, neither in his lifetime, nor after his death, neither at any place nor any time, and that the only one who influences the affairs is Allaah, alone, the One free of all defect and blemish. So it is very clear from this that he is accusing the *Salafees* of believ-

---

142. It is an established *hadeeth* having a number of chains and witness in the *Mu'jams* of at-Tabaraanee and other sources. Al-Mundhiree indicates in *at-Targheeb* (3/26) that it is *hasan* and I have quoted it and researched it in *as-Saheehah* (no.2998).

ing that the Prophet (ﷺ) had personal influence over the affairs during his lifetime. However this is a clear lie and an open slander, no *Salafee* ever says this. Indeed no such thing ever crosses the minds of the *Salafees*. Indeed how could they say this when they are the callers to pure *tawheed* and to the correct religion. They are those who give their greatest concern to making their worship purely for Allaah, the Most High, alone, and to purify their beliefs from every taint of *shirk*, and from everything detrimental to *Tawheed*, even if it is just a mistake in wording. Then upon this way they are faced with harm from the people, defamation, slanders and foul accusations. But the people and amongst them Dr. al-Bootee only have malice for them because of their true call. Despite this he is not afraid to accuse them of their false and futile charge which even he, as we believe, before anyone else knows to be slander. Otherwise let him explain to us, if he can, the source of this alleged saying, and who from the *Salafees* had said it, and in which of their books or publications it is quoted. If he does not do so, and how will he be able to, then his falsehood and false accusations will be clear for all to see.

Something else that should be mentioned here are the words of al-Bootee: "And whoever claims anything from that is an Unbeliever by consensus of the Muslims." So what this saying amounts to (along with his claim in the previous point), if carefully considered is a general declaration of Unbelief against all the *Salafees*. This is a further lie and an oppressive accusation. There is no doubt that Allaah will bring him to account for it, since the *Salafees* are Muslims. Indeed they are the people who have the most right to the attribute of *Islaam*. They also know for certain that declaring that the Prophet (ﷺ) himself or any other person has an influence over the affairs is *shirk* with regard to Allaah's Lordship and takes a person out of the religion. They are amongst the most attentive of people to this point and those who most warn against it. Whereas al-Bootee and his ilk find various different excuses and justifications for those who fall into it. It should not be the case that we miss the opportunity to remind him and his like of what we have already mentioned in this treatise, with regard to the true reason, which leads us to prevent *tawassul* by means of persons, station and status of the pious, and it is that it is something not report-ed or found in the pure *Sharee'ah*. Nor was it done by the Prophet (ﷺ) nor his Companions. So it is, therefore, a novelty and an innovation. The texts used by those who disagree are either authentic texts which, do not show what they claim, or others are inauthentic, and this has preceded in detail.

This is the reason that causes us to deny this form of *tawassul* and we clearly say: If it were reported in the *Sharee'ah* then we would accept it and have it as our saying, and nothing would prevent us from it since we are proud by the *Sharee'ah*. Whatever it allows for us, we allow it, and whatever it forbids us from, then we forbid it. It is very strange how the Dr. ignores this fundamen-tal reason and instead invents a reason himself which his own desires delude him with. He then uses it as a means to attack and vilify us, and to incite the common people against us. So look, may Allaah have mercy upon you, at these strange manners which contradict religion and knowledge, and lament to Allaah, the Mighty and Majestic, of the fact that the truth and its people are indeed strangers in this age.

4. HIS ERROR IN CLAIMING THAT THE REASON FOR *TAWASSUL* BY MEANS OF THE PROPHET (ﷺ) IS THAT HE IS THE MOST EXCELLENT OF EVERYTHING IN CREATION.

This is a further error which the Dr. has fallen into as a result of his rashness and failure to think carefully about what he writes. He declares that the reason for *tawassul* by means of the Prophet (ﷺ) is that he is without restriction the best of all created beings to Allaah, and also that he is a mercy from Allaah for all the servants, as we have already mentioned. So we say to him: That in your view this means, therefore, that as for one who is not that, (i.e. not the most excellent of the creation to Allaah...), that it is not permissible to use him for *tawassul*, since the reason which allows it is absent in such a person. This is because, if this is the reason and condition for it, then when it is absent, what-ever depends upon it must also be absent. So the meaning of his words, even if he himself does not comprehend what he says, is that it is not permissible to make *tawassul* by means of anyone except the Prophet (ﷺ). But we know for certain that he believes something contrary to this, and he allows *tawassul* by means of every prophet, pious servant loved by Allaah, or righteous person. So he himself is saying something which he does not believe, and is contradicting himself. The reason for this is one of two things: Either he does not understand what the term *manaat* (reason behind something, that upon which it is conditional) means with the scholars, or he has not considered what is a direct consequence of his speech, and this is the more likely, and Allaah knows best.

Something else that we should mention at this point is as is affirmed by the scholars of the principle of *Fiqh* - that for something to be accepted as being a reason behind some ruling, upon which it is conditional, it must be something specified in a text of the Book or the *Sunnah*, and it cannot be based upon supposition or extracted through personal deduction. But if we look at the words of the Dr. then we find that he claims something to be such a reason, for which there is not even anything resembling a proof in the Book or the *Sunnah*. Rather his basis for it is mere supposition and surmise. So is this the manner in which the Dr. thinks that knowledge and *Sharee'ah* realities are affirmed, he who has headed some of his books with the phrase: "Treatise at the pinnacle of research"?

A third and final matter is that the Dr.'s claims that the Prophet (ﷺ) is the most excellent of all created beings with Allaah, and this is a matter of belief and creed (*'aqeedah*) *and in his view* such things cannot be established[143] except through a text whose establishment is definite due to its having no possibility of error, and whose meaning is also clear and unequivocal[144] i.e. by an *Aayah* whose meaning is clear and unequivocal, or by a *hadeeth* which is

---

143. As he has affirmed in more than one of his books, for example *Kubral-Yaqeenaat al-Kawniyyah* (p.26, second edn.) and *al-Laamadhhabiyyah*.

144. To see the error of this opinion refer to my book: 'The *Hadeeth* is a Proof itself in Rulings and Beliefs.'

mutawaatir in transmission and also clear and unequivocal in meaning. So where is such a text to establish that he (ﷺ) is the most unrestrictedly excellent of all created beings to Allaah? As is known this is matter about which there is disagreement between the scholars, Imaam Aboo Haneefah, *rahimahullaah*, withheld about this matter, not expressing a view, and whoever wishes to research into it further should refer to *Sharhut-Tahawiyyah*, the explanation of Imaam Ja'far at-Tahaawee al-Hanafee's, *rahimahullaah*, book of *'Aqeedah* (pp. 337-348, Maktabul-Islaamee edn., with my checking). Then perhaps the Dr.'s basis for affirming this point of *'aqeedah* is what occurs in a story relating to the Ascension (*al-Mi'raaj*) which is falsely and treacherously attributed to the noble Companion 'Abdullaah ibn 'Abbaas, *radiyallaahu 'anhumaa*, despite the fact that al-Bootee himself says[145] about the story in question: "It is a book which has been concocted by bringing together baseless and futile *ahaadeeth* which have no basis and no chain of narration"! In reality his own words here as they stand are futile, since the book in question does actually bring many authentic *ahaadeeth* also, some of them from the narrations reported by both al-Bukhaaree and Muslim. However the author mixes them up with other *ahaadeeth*, some of which are fabricated and others have no basis, and other are weak. I have explained this in my reply to Dr. al-Bootee which was published in *at-Tamaddun al-Islaamee* magazine and then later as an independent treatise as has preceded.

5.   HIS IGNORANCE OF THE LANGUAGE MEANING OF 'SEEKING FOR SOMEONE TO INTERCEDE ON ONES BEHALF' (*ISTISHFAA'*).

This is a further atrocious mistake which the Dr. has fallen into may Allaah correct and guide him, in that he uses the term *istishfaa'* (seeking for someone to intercede on ones behalf), which occurs in the *ahaadeeth* about the Prayer for seeking rain, as a proof for the innovated form of *tawassul*. So he said: "The recommendation for seeking intercession from the righteous and pious people and those in the prophet's (ﷺ) family, which is reported with regard to

---

145. In his book *Fiqhus-Seerah* (p.155).

the Rain-Prayer and elsewhere, has already been mentioned. This is something about which there is consensus of the vast majority of imaams and scholars, amongst them ash-Shawkaanee, Ibn Qudaamah, as-San'aanee and others." So the Dr. would not fall into such an error if he understood the language meaning of *istishfaa'*. In order to enlighten the readers and benefit them I will quote what some of the books of the language say in explanation of it. The author of *al-Qaamoosul-Muheet* said: "*ash-Shaf*: (Even number) is what is contrary to 'odd', and it is what completes a pair. So *ash-Shafa'ah* is to add someone else and bring him along with you when you are seeking something. A sheep described as *Shaafi'* is a ewe with one lamb in her belly for a pair. Then *istishfaa'* means: to request someone to make a pair with you." In *al-Mu'jamul-Waseet* produced by the Arabic language institute in Egypt there occurs: "When something is made *Shaf* it means that something is added to it to make it a pair... and *istashfa'a* means: he sought after someone to aid him, and *ash-Shafee'* and *ash-Shafaai'* are pairs, and *ash-Shafaa'ah* is the words of ones partner, and *ash-Shafee'* is one who joins another and forms a pair."

In *an-Nihaayah* of Ibnul-Atheer there occurs: "*ash-Shuf'ah* is derived from increase since *ash-Shafee'* is one who adds an article on sale to what he possesses and so makes it a partner of it, as it were originally single but became a pair due to the addition of the *Shaf*. The person who is *ash-Shaafi'* is the one who makes that which is odd even..."

From these quotes and their like the meaning of *istishfaa'* is very clear and it is to request another person to become a partner with you in what you are seeking, so that you become a pair. So from this original language meaning the *Sharee'ah* meaning is derived. This is that you seek from the people of knowledge and the righteous that they should make supplication to Allaah along with the Muslims, at times of calamity, and so adds to the number of those who are supplicating, and so that it is hoped that the supplication will be more liable to be answered. Therefore through this we can understand what the 'Greater Intercession' (*ash-Shafaa'atul-Uzmaa*) for the Prophet (ﷺ) on the

Day of Resurrection is. Indeed it is, by agreement of the scholars, the supplication of the Prophet (ﷺ) for the people after they have come to him and asked him to supplicate to Allaah, the Most High, to hasten the Reckoning for them. None of the People of knowledge have understood from this that the people should say, for example,: "O Allaah because of the station which Muhammad (ﷺ) had with You hasten the Reckoning for us." What is truly strange is that Dr. al-Bootee should have the audacity to claim that there is consensus of the imaams and scholars, amongst them ash-Shawkaanee, Ibn Qudaamah and as-San'aanee upon his strange and irregular understanding which is based upon severe ignorance of the meaning of terms used in the language and the *Sharee'ah*. We will suffice in replying to him by quoting the words of just one of those imaams whose name he used and whom he claimed shared his understanding of *istishfaa'*, meaning, Imaam Ibn Qudaamah al-Maqdisee who wrote the largest book of Hanbalee *fiqh* '*Al-Mughnee*'. He says in it (2/295): "It is recommended to seek rain by means of one who is seen to be righteous, since that will mean that the supplication is more liable to be answered. Indeed 'Umar sought rain by means of al-'Abbaas, the uncle of the Prophet (ﷺ). Ibn 'Umar said: "In the year of drought and destruction 'Umar sought rain by means of al-'Abbaas,. He said: 'O Allaah this is the uncle of Your Prophet and we turn to You by means of him, so grant us rain,' and Allaah quickly granted them rain." It is also reported that Mu'aawiyah went out to pray for rain, so when he sat upon the minbar he said: "Where is Yazeed ibn al-Aswad al-Jurashee?" So Yazeed stood up, and Mu'aawiyah supplicated and sat Yazeed at his feet, then he said: "O Allaah we use the best of us and the most excellent of us, Yazeed ibn al-Aswad to intercede on our behalf," then he said: "O Yazeed raise up your hands," so he raised up his hands and supplicated to Allaah, the Most High. So large clouds like a shield appeared from the west, and the wind blew and they were blessed with such an amount of rain that they could hardly reach their homes. Another time ad-Dahhaak also sought rain by means of him."

So it is very clear from the words of Ibn Qudaamah that what he means by the *istishfaa'* reported in the *hadeeth* about the Rain-Prayer is that the ruler of the Muslims should request someone from the people of knowledge and piety to supplicate along with the Muslims, turning to their Lord, the One free of all-imperfections, that He should remove distress from His Believing servants. Ibn Qudaamah did not mean, and we can be certain that there never even crossed his mind, the like of this erroneous understanding which al-Bootee and the innovators like him seek to apply to *Sharee'ah* wordings. Do you not see how al-Bootee claims the like of this counterfeit consensus and then seeks to declare Ibn Qudaamah and others to be witnesses to that. But here are the words of Ibn Qudaamah, which totally uproot his false understanding. Maybe it is that he is unable to understand what is written in the books, or perhaps it is the case that he makes whatever claims he wishes without even referring to the books at all. Perhaps it is the case that he feels safe that his readers will merely blindly accept whatever he tells them, and that no one amongst them will check, or read for themselves to verify what is being said? Indeed this is very regrettable, by Allaah, and one of the greatest calamities which we see in the life of Muslims. It is also, without a doubt, one of the greatest causes of the backwardness of the Muslims, their weakness, and their decline. It is also impossible to change this condition unless they change their indifference and rigidness, their following of Sufism, their rigid following of single *madhhabs*, and their acceptance of theological rhetoric and logic in matters of belief. It will not be possible until they leave all of these things found in them and return to the true guidance as found in the Book and the *Sunnah*, and which is manifest by the pure and radiant *Salafee da'wah*.

6. HIS ERROR IN CLAIMING THAT THE BLIND MAN'S *TAWASSUL* WAS BY MEANS OF THE STATION OF THE PROPHET(ﷺ) WITH ALLAAH.

We complete our reply to Dr. al-Bootee by drawing attention to his error in claiming that the *tawassul* of the blind man was by means of the station of the Prophet (ﷺ), and by means of his status as the most excellent of the creation to Allaah. Indeed this is merely a claim and has no proof to support it, and the

Dr. cannot even bring something resembling proof to establish it. Rather it has preceded in this treatise that the *tawassul* of the blind-man was by means of the supplication of the Prophet (ﷺ). We have also refuted all the doubts that we are aware of raised by the antagonists and which they use as evidence for their erroneous view. We have likewise explained the weakness of the addition to the *hadeeth* quoted by the Dr. which he remained silent about either due to ignorance or feigning ignorance, and that is the saying: "So whenever you have a need then do the same." So we will not repeat that for fear of prolonging the matter further.

From all that has preceded it will be clear to every just person who desires the truth that these doubts which are raised are baseless and futile. Indeed Allaah, the Blessed and Most High, says:

$$ بَلْ نَقْذِفُ بِالْحَقِّ عَلَى الْبَٰطِلِ فَيَدْمَغُهُ فَإِذَا هُوَ زَاهِقٌ وَلَكُمُ الْوَيْلُ مِمَّا تَصِفُونَ $$

"Nay, We fling the truth against the falsehood (disbelief), so it destroys it, and behold, it (falsehood) is vanished. And woe to you for that which you ascribe (to Us)."[146]

He says:

$$ وَلَا يَأْتُونَكَ بِمَثَلٍ إِلَّا جِئْنَاكَ بِالْحَقِّ وَأَحْسَنَ تَفْسِيرًا ۝ $$

"And no example or similitude do they bring, but We reveal to you the truth, and the better explanation thereof."[147]

---

146. Soorah Al-Anbiyaa (21): 18
147. Soorah Al-Furqaan(25): 33

All praise and thanks are for Allaah at the beginning and the end for His grant-ing and guiding to what is correct and good. He alone is the One Whose aid we seek. None has the right to be worshipped except Him, and there is no Lord but Him. O Allaah how free and far removed You are from every defect and blemish and all praises are for You. I testify that none has the right to be worshipped except You. I ask for Your forgiveness and turn in repentance to You.

GLOSSARY

Aayah (pl. Aayaat): a Sign of Allaah; a verse of the Qur'aan.

Aayaat: See *Aayah*.

'Abd: worshipper.

Aboo (Abee, Abaa): father of; used as a means of identification.

Adhaan: call to Prayer.

'Alaihis-salaam: "may Allaah protect and preserve him." It is said after the name of a Prophet of Allaah or after the name of an angel.

Ahaadeeth: See *Hadeeth*.

Ansaar: "Helpers"; the Muslims of Madeenah who supported the Muslims who migrated from Makkah.

'Aqeedah: that which binds or that which is rooted in the heart; the principles and details of belief.

Companions (Ar. *Sahaabah*): the Muslims who saw the Prophet (ﷺ) and died upon Islaam.

Da'eef: weak; unauthentic (narration).

Eemaan: faith; to affirm all that was revealed to the Messenger (ﷺ), affirming with the heart, testifying with the tongue and acting with the limbs. The actions of the limbs are from the completeness of *Eemaan*. Faith increases with obedience to Allaah and decreases with disobedience.

Fiqh: the understanding and application of the *Sharee'ah* from its sources.

Haraam: prohibited under the *Sharee'ah*.

Ibn: son of; used as a means of identification.

Ijmaa': "consensus"; a unified opinion of scholars regarding a certain issue.

Ijtihaad: exertion of effort; the process of arriving at a reasoned decision by a scholar on an issue.

Imaam: leader; leader in *Salaah*, knowledge or *fiqh*; leader of a state.

Isnaad: the chain of narrators linking the collector of the saying to the person quoted.

Jinn: a creation of Allaah created from smokeless fire.

Jumu'ah: Friday.

Kaafir (pl. *Kuffaar*): a rejector of Islaam i.e. a disbeliever.

Khaleefah (pl. *Khulafaa'*): the head of the Islamic government (the *khilaafah*) to whom the oath of allegiance is given.

Khilaafah: the Islamic state.

Khulafaa': see *khaleefah*.

Khutbah: sermon.

Kufr: Disbelief.

Madhhab: position or opinion of a scholar; school of thought.

Marfoo': raised; a narration attributed to the Prophet (ﷺ).

Mawdoo': fabricated; spurious; invented (narration).

Mawqoof: stopped; a narration from a Companion (not going back to the Prophet (ﷺ)).

Minbar: pulpit.

Mu'adhdhin: one who performs the *adhaan*.

Mujtahid: One who is qualified to pass judgements using *ijtihaad*.

Mursal: loose; a narration in which a Successor narrated directly from the Prophet (ﷺ), i.e. omitting the Companion from who he heard it.

Mushrik: one who worships others along with Allaah or ascribes one or more of Allaah's attributes to other than Him; one who commits shirk.

Mustahabb: recomended; one who does a mustahabb action is rewarded, but one who leaves it is not punished.

Mutawaatir: a *hadeeth* which is narrated by a very large number of reporters, such that it cannot be supposed that that they all agreed upon a lie.

Qiblah: the direction the Muslims face during prayer (i.e. towards Makkah).

Radiyallaahu 'anhu/'anhaa/'anhum/'anhumaa: may Allaah be pleased with him/her/them/both of them.

Rahimahullaah/Rahimahumullaah: may Allaah bestow His mercy upon him/them.

Rak'ah: one cycle of the Prayer, consisting of standing, bowing and prostrating.

Rukoo': "bowing," a part of the prayer.

Saheeh: correct; an authentic narration.

Salaat: prescribed prayer (e.g. the five obligatory prayers); prayers upon the Prophet (ﷺ).

Salaf: predecessors; the early Muslims; the Muslims of the first three generations: the Companions, the Successors and their successors.

Salafee: one who ascribes himself to the salaf and follows in their way.

Salafus-Saaliheen: pious predecessors; the Muslims of the first three generations: the Companions, the Successors and their successors.

Shaadh: unusual; a narration whose narrators are reliable but they contradict that which is better established and more authentic.

Shaikh: scholar.

Sharee'ah: the Divine code of Law.

Shawaal: the tenth month of the Islamic calendar. It is the month after *Ramadaan*.

Shirk: assocciating partners with Allaah; compromising any aspect of *tawheed*.

Soorah: a Chapter of the Qur'aan.

Sufism: Originally applied to people who devoted themselves to solitary devotions remaining aloof from the world to an extreme degree. In time they introduced various innovated practices and developed into various tareeqahs, very similar to the monastic orders, each following their own innovated and special way, incorporating many aspects of shirk and kufr. See "The Reality of Sufism in Light of the Qur'aan and *Sunnah*" by Shaykh Muhammad ibn Rabee' al-Madkhalee (Al-Hidaayah Publishing and Distribution, U.K., 1995).

Sujood: "prostration," a part of the prayer.

Sunnah: in its broadest sense, the entire *Deen* which the Prophet (ﷺ) came with and taught, i.e. all matters of belief, rulings, manners and actions which were conveyed by the Companions. It also includes those matters which the Prophet (ﷺ) established by his sayings, actions and tacit approval - as opposed to *bid'ah* (innovation).

Sunnah: an action of the Prophet (ﷺ).

Taabi'ee (pl. *Taabi'een*): a Muslim (other than another Companion) who met a Companion.

Taabi'een: see taabi'ee.

Tafseer: explanation of the Qur'aan.

Taqleed: to follow someone's opinion without an evidence.

Taqwa: "*taqwa* is acting in obedience to Allaah, hoping for His mercy upon light from Him and Taqwa is leaving acts of disobedience, out of fear of Him, upon light from Him."

Tawheed: Allaah is the only Lord of creation, He alone, is their provider and sustainer, Allaah has Names and Attributes that none of the creation share and Allaah is to be singled out for worship, alone. *Tawheed* is maintaining the Oneness of Allaah in all the above mentioned categories. Islaam makes a clear distinction between the Creator and the created.

Ummah: "nation"; the Muslims as a group.

Wudoo': the ablution (ritual washing) that is performed before the Prayer and certain other acts of worship.